# What on Earth is an SAP® IDoc?

Jelena Perfiljeva

# Thank you for purchasing this book from Espresso Tutorials!

Like a cup of espresso coffee, Espresso Tutorials SAP books are concise and effective. We know that your time is valuable and we deliver information in a succinct and straightforward manner. It only takes our readers a short amount of time to consume SAP concepts. Our books are well recognized in the industry for leveraging tutorial-style instruction and videos to show you step by step how to successfully work with SAP.

Check out our YouTube channel to watch our videos at
https://www.youtube.com/user/EspressoTutorials.

If you are interested in SAP Finance and Controlling, join us at
http://www.fico-forum.com/forum2/
to get your SAP questions answered and contribute to discussions.

## Related titles from Espresso Tutorials:

▶ Boris Rubarth: First Steps in ABAP®
  http://5015.espresso-tutorials.com

▶ Antje Kunz: SAP® Legacy System Migration Workbench (LSMW)
  http://5051.espresso-tutorials.com

▶ Darren Hague: Universal Worklist with SAP NetWeaver® Portal
  http://5076.espresso-tutorials.com

▶ Michal Krawczyk: SAP® SOA Integration
  http://5077.espresso-tutorials.com

▶ Dominique Alfermann, Stefan Hartmann, Benedikt Engel:
  SAP® HANA Advanced Modeling
  http://4110.espresso-tutorials.com

▶ Kathi Kones: SAP List Viewer (ALV) – A Practical Guide for
  ABAP Developers
  http://5112.espresso-tutorials.com

Jelena Perfiljeva
**What on Earth is an SAP® IDoc?**

| | |
|---|---|
| **ISBN:** | 978-1-5237-9740-0 |
| **Editor:** | Lisa Jackson |
| **Cover Design:** | Philip Esch, Martin Munzel |
| **Cover Photo:** | fotolia # 8083048 © Vladislav Kochelaevs |
| **Interior Design:** | Johann-Christian Hanke |

All rights reserved.

1st Edition 2016, Gleichen

© 2016 by Espresso Tutorials GmbH

**URL**: *www.espresso-tutorials.com*

**Feedback**
We greatly appreciate any kind of feedback you have concerning this book. Please mail us at *info@espresso-tutorials.com*.

# Table of Contents

# Preface

Dear Reader,

When I learned about IDocs about 10 years ago, my first thought was: "What on earth is this?!" It must be one of the most bizarre and frequently misunderstood concepts in the SAP world: complex yet simple at the same time.

This older than Internet technology is omnipresent in most SAP implementations and supports many vital interfaces. I would be lying if I said the IDoc subject was easy and fun. But knowing what it really is, how it works, and how we can use it to our advantage is a darn good skill to have for any SAP professional today and in the future.

The book you are about to enjoy is written based on my personal experience with a variety of the IDoc interfaces. My approach to knowledge sharing is simple and practical. If the information does not help you to gain a better understanding of the subject, get better results in your IDoc implementation, or at least provide some entertainment—it is not here.

Both technical and functional SAP professionals can benefit from this book. My ABAP colleagues will find the enhancement tips, as well as testing and monitoring tools useful. The functional specialists will find all the necessary configuration steps they need, including an overview of output configuration and troubleshooting tips (not usually mentioned in other publications).

Due to the IDoc subject nature, this book requires some basic knowledge of fundamental SAP concepts, such as navigation and transport system. If you are not yet familiar with SAP I suggest starting with another Espresso Tutorials book *First Steps in SAP* by Sydnie McConnell and Martin Munzel.

Now let's begin.

We have added a few icons to highlight important information. These include:

**Tips**

Tips highlight information concerning more details about the subject being described and/or additional background information.

**Attention**

Attention notices draw attention to information that you should be aware of when you go through the examples from this book on your own.

Finally, a note concerning the copyright: All screenshots printed in this book are the copyright of SAP SE. All rights are reserved by SAP SE. Copyright pertains to all SAP images in this publication. For simplification, we will not mention this specifically underneath every screenshot.

# 1 Meet the IDocs

In this chapter, readers meet the IDocs and learn about the main parts of an IDoc interface, IDoc anatomy, and different kinds of segments. Then, we will ponder whether an answer to "what is the difference between EDI and ALE?" exists and discuss when using an IDoc interface is most practical.

**Know thy SAP navigation**

Even though this book was written with beginners in mind, the activities you need to perform require at least basic knowledge of SAP navigation and functionality. For example, you should already know how to navigate between the screens and use the most common standard functions, such as Save (🖫) or Execute (🕀).

## 1.1 Definitions

Every academic book begins with a rather long chapter on definitions and other important, but super boring stuff. I do not like that at all and always end up flipping past those pages to get to juicier parts with the screenshots. After all, as Alice once wisely noted: "…and what is the use of a book without pictures or conversations?" *("Alice's Adventures in Wonderland", by Lewis Carroll)*.

Indeed. So why don't I just show you an IDoc instead of talking about it? Here it is (see Figure 1.1):

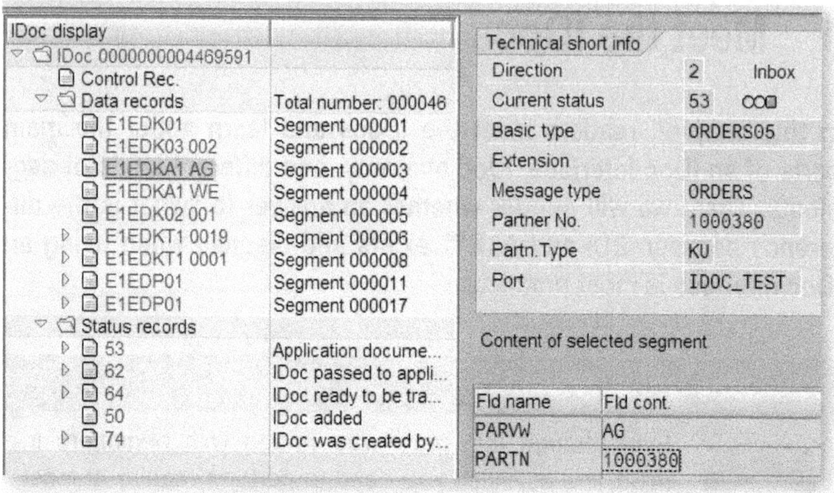

| IDoc display | | | Technical short info | | |
|---|---|---|---|---|---|
| ▽ ⬜ IDoc 0000000004469591 | | | Direction | 2 | Inbox |
| ⬜ Control Rec. | | | Current status | 53 | ∞⬚ |
| ▽ ⬜ Data records | Total number: 000046 | | Basic type | ORDERS05 | |
| ⬜ E1EDK01 | Segment 000001 | | Extension | | |
| ⬜ E1EDK03 002 | Segment 000002 | | | | |
| ⬜ E1EDKA1 AG | Segment 000003 | | Message type | ORDERS | |
| ⬜ E1EDKA1 WE | Segment 000004 | | Partner No. | 1000380 | |
| ⬜ E1EDK02 001 | Segment 000005 | | Partn.Type | KU | |
| ▷ ⬜ E1EDKT1 0019 | Segment 000006 | | Port | IDOC_TEST | |
| ▷ ⬜ E1EDKT1 0001 | Segment 000008 | | | | |
| ▷ ⬜ E1EDP01 | Segment 000011 | | Content of selected segment | | |
| ▷ ⬜ E1EDP01 | Segment 000017 | | | | |
| ▽ ⬜ Status records | | | | | |
| ▷ ⬜ 53 | Application docume... | | Fld name | Fld cont. | |
| ▷ ⬜ 62 | IDoc passed to appli... | | PARVW | AG | |
| ▷ ⬜ 64 | IDoc ready to be tra... | | PARTN | 1000380 | |
| ⬜ 50 | IDoc added | | | | |
| ▷ ⬜ 74 | IDoc was created by... | | | | |

Figure 1.1: IDoc example

It probably looks unimpressive and somewhat confusing at the same time, so maybe skipping the definitions isn't the best idea after all, huh? Let's go over some basics then, shall we?

It is important to understand that **IDoc is just a data container in SAP**. It does not have any magical powers and cannot solve any issues with business process, or other technical interface challenges. But it can take data from point A to point B relatively consistently and does have some nice bonus features.

## IDoc display

 You can view IDoc using transaction codes **WE02** and **WE05**. There is no significant difference between these two transactions and they both are assigned to the same program.

With this in mind, it is reasonable to ask—if IDoc is just a container, how does it get into SAP and what does it do?

Great question! (That's what people usually say when they have already prepared a very clever answer.) IDocs cannot do anything by themselves and usually they are part of some interface. What is the interface, you ask? Well, when two computer systems love each other very, very much... um... they might want to exchange some information.

For example, when a purchase order is created in System A, it might want to tell System B that a sales order needs to be created. And, to be nice, System B then sends a confirmation back to System A ("yep, got your order!") and then later a shipping notification. So, when System A has some information, how does it send it to System B and vice versa? (Assume that in this example System B is an SAP system, so it is the one we care about.) There are different ways to do that. To define how exactly these systems will communicate, in System B (SAP) we would create *a port* (Figure 1.2).

More detail on that later but, for example, a port could point to an XML file, or a *remote connection* (called "RFC connection" in SAP). Remote connection is a way for two systems to "talk" to each other.

---

### Inbound and outbound interfaces

 The interfaces can either be inbound or outbound depending on whether they bring data into the SAP system (inbound) or take it out of it (outbound).

---

| Port | XMLFILE |
|---|---|
| Description | XML File |

XML format
- ○ SAP Release 46
- ◉ Unicode

| Outbound file | Outbound: Trigger |
|---|---|

- ○ Logical directory          📭 Access test
- ◉ physical directory

| Directory | D:\usr\sap\put |
|---|---|
| Function module | |
| Description | |
| Outbound file | idoc_document.xml |

*Figure 1.2: Port example*

The communication part is rather simple and now we arrive at more complex questions: how does System B know what System A is sending it and what to send back? Also, how does it create an order? Is there some kind of BAPI, or a Z program? How would it know Ship-to and Sold-to? And the material number—wouldn't System A send its own? And how does it send a confirmation? Does it track changes in the sales order? Isn't it very complicated? Okay, okay, hold your horses. This is just the definition section, there are over 100 pages to go. We will get there, I promise.

The next part of the interface in SAP is called the *partner profile* (see Figure 1.3). There are different types of partners available (customer, vendor, and logical system to name a few). For this example, we would either choose customer type (because we are dealing with a customer in System A), or logical system (because, well, it is a system). We will explore the differences in Chapter 2.

## Transaction codes: port and partner profile

 Port is defined in transaction **WE21** and partner profile in transaction **WE20**. If you feel it would be more logical to have these transactions in reverse order (because port is defined first) you are not alone.

In the newly created partner profile, we would specify that we expect to receive from this partner the sales orders and we will send back the order confirmations and shipment notifications.

How would we do that? Oh, this brings us to a very interesting subject: message type and IDoc type. Since there are at least a dozen completely different meanings the words "message" and "type" might have in SAP, this used to confuse me a lot. You can easily find the official definitions in the SAP documentation, but I will give you my own, simpler ones.

*Message type* defines the general type of information, or business transaction. For example, sales and purchase orders share the same message type ORDERS in SAP and material master data is assigned the MATMAS message type.

*IDoc type* defines the specific IDoc data structure.

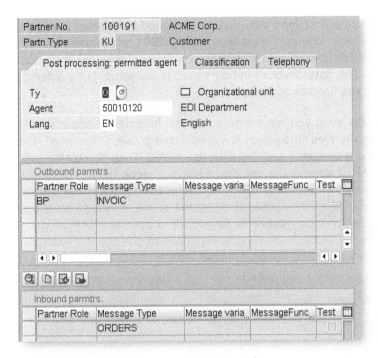

*Figure 1.3: Partner profile example (customer)*

When I first learned about these two types, my initial reaction was: why do we need two different kinds of "types"? An order is order, and material master is material master. Isn't it already obvious from the message type what kind of information we are dealing with?

There are a few reasons for having separate message and IDoc types.

▶ Two words: backwards compatibility. New features may be intro-duced all the time, but no one wants to break the interfaces al-ready in use. If we had two SAP systems with different versions and their definitions of the same IDoc did not match, that would be a problem. For this reason, instead of changing an existing IDoc type, SAP creates new IDoc types when necessary. That is how we end up with ORDERS01, ORDERS02, etc.

▶ Different IDoc types may be assigned to the same message type to allow for slightly different "flavors" of the same transaction.

13

▶ The same IDoc type also may be assigned to different message types. For example, IDoc type ORDERS01 is assigned to both ORDERS (order) and ORDRSP (order confirmation) message type. The data structure in both cases is the same, but a different business function is performed.

So, let's review what you have learned so far. Information departs from System A and arrives to System B via something called "the port", the partner profile is checked, and the IDoc is created. Then something gets posted in SAP. It seems like we are missing a piece here... Naturally, there is no magic in SAP, only ABAP, so the missing piece is transaction **WE57** where a function module is assigned to the message type and IDoc type. The function module is essentially a special ABAP program that executes the process the IDoc is supposed to perform (for example, creates a sales order or a material master record).

---

**Where to find function modules**

 Function modules may be viewed in transaction **SE37** or **SE80**.

---

Similarly, when data goes back from System B to System A, a special ABAP program runs and takes care of the data transfer to an IDoc. That's the process in a nutshell. Outbound interfaces are covered in more detail in Chapter 3 and inbound interfaces in Chapter 4.


## 1.2   IDoc anatomy

An IDoc consists of three main parts:

▶ Control record
▶ Data records (segments)
▶ Status records

The *control record* (see Figure 1.4) contains general information about the IDoc: its unique number, direction, type, partner number, etc.

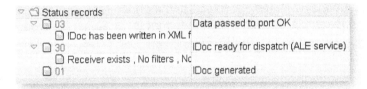

Figure 1.4: IDoc control record

Status records (Figure 1.5) are like the IDoc's travel journal—they keep track of the IDoc's journey through the hills and valleys (or dungeons?) of SAP.

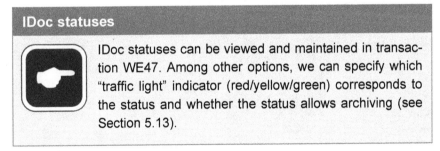

Figure 1.5: IDoc status record

Status (two-digit number) can be used to filter the IDocs conveniently. For example, the person in charge of monitoring an IDoc interface might need to pay attention to the IDocs with status 51 (error).

### IDoc statuses

IDoc statuses can be viewed and maintained in transaction WE47. Among other options, we can specify which "traffic light" indicator (red/yellow/green) corresponds to the status and whether the status allows archiving (see Section 5.13).

Data records contain—you guessed it!—the actual data that the IDoc transfers.

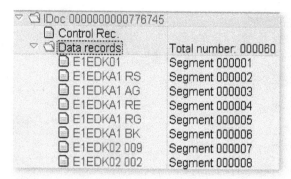

Figure 1.6: IDoc data records

In Figure 1.6 you can see some mysterious letter and number combinations, such as E1EDK01. Those are the *segment names,* aka *segment types.* Each segment can contain multiple fields filled with data and the segments may also form a parent-child hierarchy.

This type of setup may look familiar to you and for good reason. There is definitely some resemblance with the XML format (after all, an IDoc can create an XML file). If you are an ABAPer you will also immediately recognize a structure and it is a great observation because each segment type is, in fact, defined as a structure in the Data Dictionary.

Let's take a closer look at some segments. Figure 1.7 shows an example of the segment E1EDK01 content. The field names are in the left column and the field content is in the right column. This is all there is to it, very simple.

| Content of Selected Segment | |
| --- | --- |
| Fld Name | Fld Cont. |
| CURCY | USD |
| HWAER | USD |
| WKURS | 1.00000 |
| ZTERM | NT30 |
| BSART | INVO |
| BELNR | 0090036353 |
| GEWEI | KGM |
| FKART_RL | LR |
| RECIPNT_NO | 0000100191 |
| FKTYP | L |

Figure 1.7: Segment E1EDK01 content example

In the Data Dictionary (transaction **SE11**) we can also see the definition of E1EDK01 structure (Figure 1.8).

| Structure | E1EDK01 | | | Active | |
|---|---|---|---|---|---|
| Short Description | IDoc: Document header general data | | | | |

Attributes  Components  Entry help/check  Currency/quantity fields

| Component | Typing Method | | Component Type | Data Type | Length | [ |
|---|---|---|---|---|---|---|
| ACTION | Types | | | CHAR | 3 | |
| KZABS | Types | | | CHAR | 1 | |
| CURCY | Types | | | CHAR | 3 | |
| HWAER | Types | | | CHAR | 3 | |
| WKURS | Types | | | CHAR | 12 | |
| ZTERM | Types | | | CHAR | 17 | |
| KUNDEUINR | Types | | | CHAR | 20 | |
| EIGENUINR | Types | | | CHAR | 20 | |

*Figure 1.8: Structure E1EDK01 in the Data Dictionary*

A keen observer would be quick to point out, "Wait a second—these two don't match!" The reason for this discrepancy is that the Data Dictionary shows the full definition of all the possible fields in the segment, but when an IDoc is displayed, only the fields with data are visible, while other (blank) fields are hidden. This is quite a nice feature because most of the time only a few fields contain any information and if blank segments were not hidden we would have to do a lot of scrolling.

We can also see that all the fields in the segment structure are of type CHAR, i.e., they are alphanumeric fields. One reason for such a definition is to avoid any kind of potential conversion errors while transferring data.

You might notice that some segments have additional identifiers next to the segment name. This happens when the same segment is used for slightly different kinds of information.

A good example would be the E1EDKA1 segment which contains the partner information. In Figure 1.6 we can see several E1EDKA1 segments with different letters (RS, AG, etc.) next to them. Every partner's data (e.g., Ship-to, Sold-to, vendor) is very similar and includes account number, address, phone, email, etc. Hence there is no need to maintain different segment types for each partner type. In such cases, a special field called a *qualifier* is added at the beginning of the segment. It acts as kind of a segment subtype.

In the case of the E1EDKA1 segment, the first field, Partner Type (PARVW) acts as a qualifier, but other segments, such as E1EDP02, have the actual field called Qualifier (QUALF) in the definition (see Figure 1.9).

| Structure | E1EDP02 | | | Active | |
|-----------|---------|---|---|--------|---|
| Short Description | IDoc: Document Item Reference Data | | | | |

Attributes  Components  Entry help/check  Currency/quantity fields

Predefined Type — 1 / 7

| Component | Typing M. | Component Type | Data | Length | Short Description |
|-----------|-----------|----------------|------|--------|-------------------|
| QUALF | Types | EDI_QUALFR | CHAR | 3 | IDOC qualifier reference document |
| BELNR | Types | EDI_BELNR | CHAR | 35 | IDOC document number |
| ZEILE | Types | EDI1082_A | CHAR | 6 | Item number |
| DATUM | Types | EDIDAT8 | CHAR | 8 | IDOC: Date |
| UZEIT | Types | EDITIM6 | CHAR | 6 | IDOC: Time |

*Figure 1.9: Segment structure definition with qualifier*

In some IDocs, you also might see "parent" segments with "child" segments underneath (see Figure 1.10). The "parent" segment (here E1EDP01) keeps segments with the data relevant to the same object together. For example, the object could be a sales order item or an invoice item.

| ▽ 🖹 E1EDP01 | Segment 000037 |
|---|---|
| 🖹 E1EDP02 001 | Segment 000038 |
| 🖹 E1EDP02 002 | Segment 000039 |
| 🖹 E1EDP02 016 | Segment 000040 |
| 🖹 E1EDP03 029 | Segment 000041 |
| 🖹 E1EDP03 011 | Segment 000042 |
| 🖹 E1EDP03 025 | Segment 000043 |
| 🖹 E1EDP03 027 | Segment 000044 |

*Figure 1.10: "Parent" and "child" segments*

## 1.3  IDoc documentation

Transaction **WE60** displays documentation for the IDoc types and segment types. To get the most out of it, some setting adjustments might be needed. (Note that WE60 may look slightly different depending on your SAP version.)

On the selection screen (Figure 1.11) enter the IDoc type (in field BASIC TYPE) or segment type (in field SEGMENT TYPE). Be sure to check the DATA RECORD checkbox.

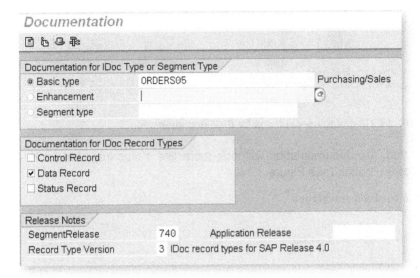

Figure 1.11: WE60 selection screen

If you execute the transaction "as is", then most likely the result will look like gibberish (see Figure 1.12).

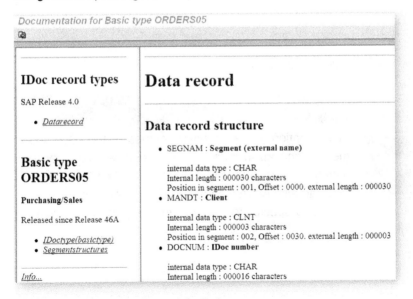

Figure 1.12: Documentation – default view

In this case, go back to the selection screen and use the menu GOTO • USER SETTINGS to check the checkboxes as shown in Figure 1.13.

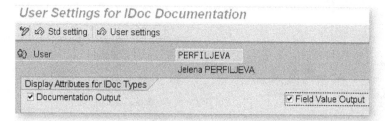

*Figure 1.13: Changing user settings for IDoc documentation*

After that, the documentation will look more like it was intended for human consumption (see Figure 1.14).

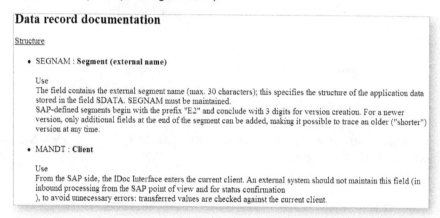

*Figure 1.14: More detailed documentation view*

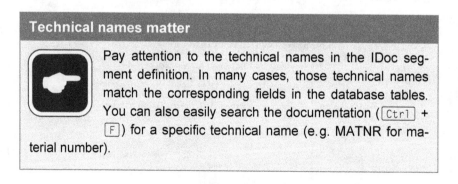

## Technical names matter

Pay attention to the technical names in the IDoc segment definition. In many cases, those technical names match the corresponding fields in the database tables. You can also easily search the documentation ( Ctrl + F ) for a specific technical name (e.g. MATNR for material number).

## 1.4    What is the deal with ALE and EDI?

Very frequently IDoc, ALE, and EDI are mentioned together, especially in job ads. We have already established that IDoc is just a data container in SAP, so what are those other two? In the SAP documentation, you will find that *EDI (Electronic Data Interchange)* and *ALE (Application Link Enabling)* are two methodologies for IDoc interface implementation. Documentation does provide some technical details on both, but does not actually explain the difference between them (both use IDocs, port, partner profile, etc.) and leaves the readers to solve the puzzle by themselves. The IDoc books take a similar route and conveniently dodge this question as well. At the same time, a few dozen unanswered questions about the differences between ALE and EDI can be found on the SCN (SAP Community Network) website scn.sap.com. Does a straightforward answer even exist?

This question is, in fact, of little importance in practice. For years, I have worked with interfaces that fit both ALE and EDI descriptions, but if you ask me which one is which I will shrug and ask why you care. I believe it is more important simply to understand how an IDoc interface (of any kind) works.

There is one notable difference, though. The EDI concept existed since the ancient mainframe times and is not an SAP proprietary term like ALE. EDI transmission is standardized globally and several standards are currently available (ANSI X12 and EDIFACT are the most commonly used ones in North America and Europe respectively).

From my experience, it is beneficial to use the term "EDI" only when it is an actual EDI interface with a partner, i.e., two companies agree to exchange documents using one of the EDI standards (in our example System A and System B could have been EDI partners). In all other cases it is perfectly fine to call it "an IDoc interface" no matter which methodology is used.

If you are interested in further ALE and EDI reading, please refer to the sources in Appendix A.

## 1.5 When to use the IDoc interfaces and when you probably should not

The important thing to understand is that the IDoc interfaces will not solve problems that they are not designed to solve. For example, if you have two systems with a very slow network in between, an IDoc interface will not make the data transfer faster. But when used appropriately, the IDoc interfaces can be quite convenient and, in fact, require very little "babysitting" (we will talk about it in Chapter 5).

Note that if you are working on EDI integration, then an IDoc interface is the best choice. SAP offers many IDocs that correspond to EDI messages and continues to support them. Also, there is a lot of information available on the SCN website on EDI topics.

Otherwise, when it comes to strategic decisions, my rule of a thumb is: check if there is a standard IDoc you could use with as little customization as possible. If there is one, cool, otherwise don't bother with IDoc and go with another kind of interface (e.g., RFC call, web service, and even good old file interface).

The reason for this is that the IDoc interfaces are great when they work out of the box. If you can fit whatever you need to do into the Procrustean bed of the SAP Standard, an IDoc interface is a perfect choice. It is a mature technology with plenty of testing, re-processing, error handling, monitoring, and archiving functionality available. And it is supported by SAP (to some extent).

But if the standard IDocs/messages cannot provide all the required functionality, then trying to make an IDoc work "your way" can turn into a nightmare. Therefore, in such cases, I always suggest very carefully evaluating whether customizing an IDoc interface will be more effective than using a different technology.

Certainly, I do not encourage anyone to run for the woods at the first sign of customization. If there are only a few custom fields needed, it may not be a big deal. (And I will talk about the IDoc enhancements in Chapter 6.) But the interface choice needs to be practical in both the short and long term.

### Outbound interfaces easier to customize

Usually the outbound interfaces lend themselves more easily to customization than the inbound ones. If you are working on an inbound interface and find that standard IDoc functionality is missing big parts, it may be best to look for an alternative solution.

But fear not—the information in this book will give you the knowledge to make the right choices in different situations.

# 2 Common IDoc interface elements

In this chapter, we will learn about the elements that are used in both inbound and outbound IDoc interfaces: port, partner profile, logical system, and distribution model. We will create the port and logical system that will be used in all further examples in this book. Depending on your preferences and experience level, you can choose to read the chapter entirely now or refer to the corresponding articles while reading about the specific interfaces in the next chapters.

## 2.1 Port definition—WE21

A communication *port* in an SAP system is quite similar to an actual sea port. Except instead of ships dropping off or picking up their cargo, it is information flowing in and out of an SAP system. And just like ships from many countries that arrive at the same sea port, one IDoc port can be used for multiple outbound and inbound interfaces.

Ports are maintained in transaction **WE21**. On the left-hand side (Figure 2.1) we can see a list of the port types.

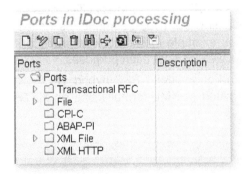

*Figure 2.1: Port types*

There is, of course, SAP documentation on the port definition but, in my opinion, it has too much information no one cares for yet lacks a clear and simple explanation of what all those port types are for. Although if SAP Help was perfect, then no one would need this book, so it is probably a good thing... Anyway, here is my "simplified" explanation of the available port types.

▶ **Transactional RFC**—This port type is used when two systems, or clients of the same SAP system, exchange data directly by establishing a remote connection and calling a special remote-enabled function (I briefly mentioned RFC in Chapter 1). The remote connection needs to be defined beforehand in transaction **SM59**. Note that the connection does not have to be between two SAP systems, it could be between an SAP system and a third-party application.

▶ **File**—This port creates a plain text file in the specified directory. The file will have the segment names at the beginning of each line followed by a stream of data (usually unreadable). This port type seems to be rarely used these days as more preference is given to RFC and XML types.

▶ **CPI-C**—This port is used for R/2 systems, which is an old version of SAP ERP.

▶ **ABAP-PI**—This port triggers a custom ABAP function. ABAP-PI is short for "ABAP Programming Interface" and has nothing to do with the SAP Process Integration solution (which has already been renamed twice and is now called SAP PRO). In the outbound interfaces, function module OWN_FUNCTION may be used as a template for the custom function. In the inbound interfaces, the custom function must call function module IDOC_INBOUND_ASYNCHRONOUS to create the IDoc.

▶ **XML file**—This port creates an XML file in the specified directory. In the XML file, you will see the IDoc segments as nodes. This port type is used as an example in this book because it is easy to deal with and works well for illustration purposes.

▶ **XML HTTP**—This port is sort of an XML / RFC hybrid. No file is created, but data is transmitted in XML format using an HTTP connection.

## What about web services?

 SAP does not provide a web service port for IDocs. One might argue that if a web service can be used, then why bother with IDocs at all? There is a great blog titled "IDoc as Web Service" on SCN by Amaresh Pani that describes a possible solution (without SAP PI/PO/PRO) and also mentions a valid business scenario in the comments (see Appendix A, page 203).

For the File and XML port types, there are two choices for the directory where the file will be created: *logical* and *physical*. What is the difference and when or why use one or the other?

## Physical directory

If we choose physical directory name then we need to enter the actual directory pathname on the application server. SAP application server directories can be viewed in transaction **AL11**. Note that some shared network directories can also be added there.

It is a good idea to check with the system administrator which directory should be used in the port definition.

Most of the examples in this book use a physical directory for simplicity, but in real life it is better to use a logical directory.

## Logical directory

If we choose the logical directory option, then we need to use a *logical file path*. Logical file paths (i.e., directory and file names) are maintained in the transaction **FILE**. In a nutshell, these paths allow the use of a neutral identifier instead of specific physical location.

Why would anyone need that? In some cases, it is convenient because we can maintain path definition once and then use the logical path name in many ports (or other places—logical paths are used all over SAP). So if the actual (i.e. "physical") directory changes then it is only necessary to make a change in only one place—logical path.

But, most importantly, logical names can be dynamic. For example, '/usr/DEV/temp' is a *static* name, but '/usr/<sysname>/temp' is *dynamic*. In the last case, <sysname> is a variable that will be filled in with the system ID, so we can conveniently use the same logical path in DEV, QAS, and PRD systems and not worry about changing it.

Logical directories take some additional effort to set up, but they can be a life saver if the path names must be changed due to a server replacement, hosting provider switch, or any other technical reason.

Also, logical directories allow for some cool customization using a function module, see Section 6.4.

> ### Beware of case sensitivity
>
>  Note that in some operating systems (OS), such as UNIX and Linux, file names are case sensitive. To find which OS is used in your SAP system, go to the menu SYSTEM • STATUS from any screen and check the OPERATING SYSTEM field.

## 2.2   Create new port—example

In this step, we will create a new port of the XML type to use in this book as an example. Naturally, any other port type can also be used in similar scenarios as needed. For example, in a real-life EDI implementation, you would most likely use an RFC port to connect to an EDI translator (see Section 3.2 for more information on the EDI interfaces).

In transaction **WE21,** select the port type XML from the list, then click the CREATE (⬜) icon. On the right-hand side, fill in the fields as shown in Figure 2.2:

▶ PORT (XMLFILE in this example) is the unique ID for the port
▶ DESCRIPTION
▶ PHYSICAL DIRECTORY or LOGICAL DIRECTORY (physical directory is used in this example)
▶ DIRECTORY—directory pathname (don't forget the slash at the end)
▶ OUTBOUND FILE—file name without extension ('.xml' extension will be added when file is created )

Technically we can leave the port name blank and have the system propose a name, but then we end up with a very "helpful" default name such as A000000002.

The last step is to click on the SAVE icon and marvel at the results of our work. Oh, wait, we almost forgot one important step. Make sure to click the ACCESS TEST button to confirm that the directory can actually be accessed. If the test is successful, you will get a message "Access to directory possible from current application server". If the test is not successful, ask a system administrator for assistance.

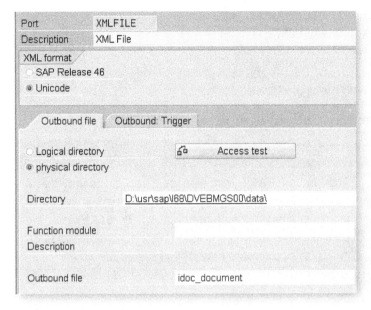

*Figure 2.2: Create new XML file port*

## 2.3 Logical system

Logical systems are defined in transaction **BD54**. Unlike the port or partner profile, this is a transportable configuration, which means the logical system must be created in a development environment and then imported into QA and production environments using *a transport request*. For more information regarding transports see SAP Help article "Change and Transport System".

Creating a new logical system is super simple. Go to transaction **BD54** and hit the [Enter] key to dismiss the warning about cross-client configuration changes. Then click on the NEW ENTRIES button and enter a unique system name and description (see Figure 2.3). In this book, we will use the same logical system SKYNET for the examples in the next chapters. (Shout out to "The Terminator" movie fans!)

Change View "Logical Systems": Overview

✏️ New Entries 🗋 🕁 🗁 🗟 🗟 🗋

| Logical Systems | |
|---|---|
| Log System | Name |
| SKYNET | Skynet |
| SMBONE | SMBONE |
| SOL_00_800 | Solution Manager CLNT 800 |

*Figure 2.3: Create new logical system*

Transport prompt will pop-up when saving the entry. Ta-dah!

## Logical systems on SALE

Transaction **SALE** can also be used to define logical systems, as well as perform other related activities. It also includes some documentation. In **SALE,** use the path BASIC SETTINGS • LOGICAL SYSTEMS • DEFINE LOGICAL SYSTEM to create new logical systems.

## 2.4  Partner profile

Partner profiles are maintained in transaction **WE20**. Visually, this transaction is very similar to WE21: the list of available options is on the left-hand side and details on the right-hand side.

In the detailed profile view (right-hand side), we can see inbound and outbound parameters. We can add or delete them by using 🔣 and 🔣 icons respectively (see Figure 2.4).

## Easy with the deletion!

Caution: if you click the 🔣 icon and confirm the deletion of the message type, it is immediately deleted from the profile. There is, unfortunately, no separate data saving step and no way to undo the deletion.

If you deleted something from an existing profile accidentally, check the profiles in another SAP system (e.g. QA if this happened in production). If you are lucky, the same configuration might still exist elsewhere and can be used to add the message type back.

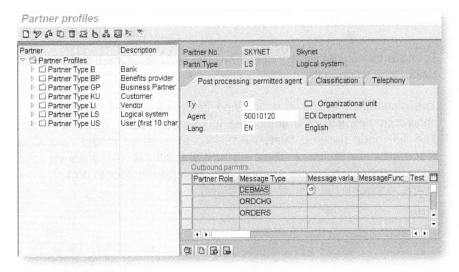

*Figure 2.4: Partner profile example*

The partner profile types are rather self-explanatory, but I find that the logical system type can cause some confusion. When do you use logical system as a partner?

Naturally, there are scenarios where simply no other partner type exists (master data, for example). In some cases, even when another partner type (e.g., customer or vendor) is available it is easier to use logical system because then we won't need to maintain a profile for every single account number. And sometimes it is simply "because I told you so"—certain SAP standard IDoc interfaces, such as inter-company billing, require specific configuration regardless of what anyone thinks about it.

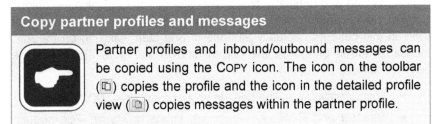

### Copy partner profiles and messages

Partner profiles and inbound/outbound messages can be copied using the COPY icon. The icon on the toolbar (🗅) copies the profile and the icon in the detailed profile view (🗅) copies messages within the partner profile.

In the next chapters, you will find more information about the partner profile setup for the specific business scenarios.

## 2.5 Distribution model

To make the logical system useful, we will need to define the *distribution model* in addition to the partner profile.

The distribution model is maintained in transaction **BD64**. Figure 2.5 shows an example of a completed inbound/outbound interface model. The first node (labeled SKYNET INTERFACES) is called *model view*. One model view can include multiple systems and interfaces. It does not have any functionality by itself; it simply acts as a placeholder to organize the interface models (very much like a folder).

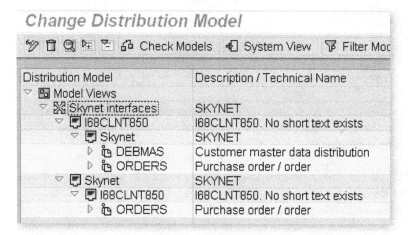

*Figure 2.5: Completed distribution model (example)*

After the model view has been created using the CREATE MODEL VIEW button, we can add message types. This seems rather illogical—wouldn't it make more sense to first add a logical system and then messages? Well, in this case it is actually all done in one step. Clicking on the ADD MESSAGE button brings up the pop-up shown in Figure 2.6. Fill in the fields as follows:

- ► MODEL VIEW NAME (the one we've just created— SKYNET)
- ► SENDER and RECEIVER—both are logical systems. For inbound interfaces, Sender is an external logical system and Receiver is the logical system assigned to the current SAP client (see transaction **SCC4**). For outbound interfaces, it's the other way around.
- ► MESSAGE TYPE—same message type as in the partner profile (e.g., ORDERS for sales or purchase orders)

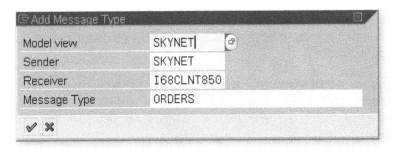

*Figure 2.6: Add message type to model view*

This seems like a lot of duplication and unnecessary entry. All of this information is also in the partner profile and, of course, we want to send and receive data in the current client. So why is this step even needed?

There are additional filters available in the distribution model for some message types (see Section 2.6). For example, we can send customer master data to the different logical systems based on the Sales Organization code. This option is not available in the partner profile.

Also, we can define the distribution model first and then generate partner profile(s) automatically from it. This is done in the same transaction **BD64** using menu ENVIRONMENT • GENERATE PARTNER PROFILES. Feel free to try it out, but I prefer to define the profiles manually. (Clearly, I have some control issues.)

We will go over the several distribution model creation examples in the next chapters.

## 2.6   Filters in the distribution model

In the distribution model view, we can add filters to ensure that only specific information is distributed. It is a simple task but the navigation is not so intuitive, so allow me to show you an example.

Suppose after some mergers and acquisitions, we end up with an SAP system that is shared by multiple organizational units. And some of them have their own external applications where they need to send the data specific only to one organization.

In this example, we will update the distribution model view for the out-bound customer master interface (see Section 3.4) to add a filter by Sales Organization.

Go to transaction **BD64** and open the model view in change mode. When we expand the model tree all the way down then underneath the message type (DEBMAS in this example), we will see the text No FILTER SET (Figure 2.7).

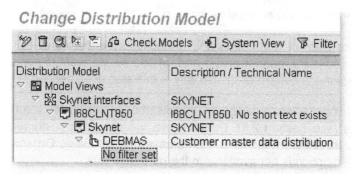

*Figure 2.7: Distribution model view without a filter*

Double-click on this text to open the CHANGE FILTER pop-up screen (Figure 2.8). In that screen, click CREATE FILTER GROUP button.

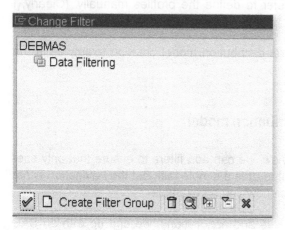

*Figure 2.8: CHANGE FILTER screen*

At first it may seem that nothing happened when you clicked it. But if you look closely, you will notice that a tiny triangle got added to the left of DATA FILTERING which, when clicked, expands the filter group (Figure 2.9).

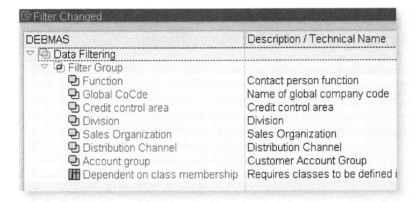

| DEBMAS | Description / Technical Name |
|---|---|
| ▽ 🗂 Data Filtering | |
| ▽ 🗂 Filter Group | |
| 🗐 Function | Contact person function |
| 🗐 Global CoCde | Name of global company code |
| 🗐 Credit control area | Credit control area |
| 🗐 Division | Division |
| 🗐 Sales Organization | Sales Organization |
| 🗐 Distribution Channel | Distribution Channel |
| 🗐 Account group | Customer Account Group |
| 🎛 Dependent on class membership | Requires classes to be defined i |

*Figure 2.9: New filter group*

In this example, we need to use the SALES ORGANIZATION field as a filter, let's double-click on it.

This opens another pop-up (Figure 2.10) to enter the specific filter values. Click the 📥 icon to add the SALES ORGANIZATION code (3000 in this example). To add more than one value, keep clicking the 📥 icon and adding. (By the way, it does look like there is a search help dropdown available for the field but, in fact, the icon does nothing. Bummer.)

*Figure 2.10: Filter Values*

Close the pop-up and the filter screen should look like Figure 2.11.

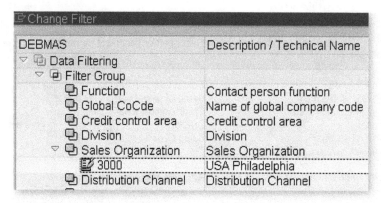

*Figure 2.11: Filter value added*

Go back to the main distribution model screen and save the entries.

Note that filters are not available for every message type.

## 2.7 Notes on IDoc display

As was mentioned in Chapter 1, IDocs are displayed in transaction **WE02** or **WE05**.

These transactions have one super-annoying quirk. In most other transactions (SP01 is a good example) if you enter the specific ID (e.g. spool number in SP01) then other selection criteria gets ignored automatically. This makes sense—if you are entering the unique ID then who cares when or by whom it was created? But in WE02 or WE05—noooo! Even when the IDoc number (unique identifier) is entered, all other criteria is still considered. And since by default the current date is set as the selection criteria, we have to change it every time when looking for a particular IDoc, unless it was created today. If we forget to do that, then the message "No documents found" is displayed—even if the IDoc number is valid.

But at least these transactions display the IDoc immediately if it is the only one that fits the selection criteria. Otherwise, we get a list of IDocs and need to select one to display in detail (Figure 2.12).

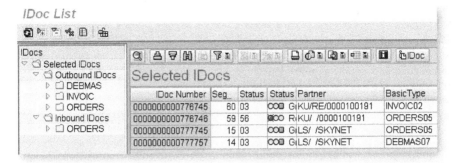

*Figure 2.12: IDoc list example*

# 3 Outbound interfaces

In this chapter, we will learn how to configure outbound IDoc interfaces for three different business scenarios. The first example will involve sending an invoice to an EDI partner. The second example will deal with the distribution of purchase orders and purchase order changes to an external system. And in the third example, we will use change pointers to send the customer master data to an external system. In each of these examples, we will use the common IDoc interface elements explained in Chapter 2.

## 3.1 Outbound interface varieties

There are different schools of thought on how to classify outbound interfaces. I feel that my own classification is quite practical.

As you know, in SAP systems we have master data (such as customer, material, and employee master records) and transactional data (orders, invoices, payments, etc.). Similarly, the IDoc interfaces can be divided into master data and transactional data. In addition, there are special implementation techniques, some of which are used more frequently than others.

Here are the main outbound interface groups, as I see them.

### Transactional data interfaces using Message Control (aka "output")

*Message Control* (MC) is the official SAP term but it is most commonly known simply as "output." This technique is available in the applications that use the condition-based output (configured in transaction NACE). Examples in this group include sales orders, purchase orders, goods movement documents, delivery documents, and others.

In these interfaces, the document output type is linked to the message type in the partner profile and the output program is used to trigger the IDoc creation. The process is very similar to sending output to a printer, but instead of a printout we get an IDoc.

The first (Section 3.2) and second (Section 3.3) interface example in this chapter belong to this group.

## Master data interfaces using the Shared Master Data tool (aka "change pointers")

The change pointer technique (frequently referred to as simply "change pointers") is part of the *Shared Master Data tool*. This technique is based on the change documents, thus you will find such interfaces where the change documents are available (customer or vendor master data, for example).

The third interface example in this chapter (Section 3.4) belongs to this group.

## Others

Specific implementation techniques for this group may vary in their degree of "funkiness." Some might use a straightforward transaction (or an ABAP report) and others might require a more complex setup. But you will find that most configuration steps needed for the first two groups also apply to this group.

For these interfaces the "devil is in the details," so it is not practical to discuss them in this book. Besides, they are usually accompanied by documentation (provided by SAP or a third-party), and I can assure you that if you can understand the simple examples in this chapter, you will have no trouble applying this knowledge to all other interfaces.

### Exercise caution with the interfaces!

 Even in the test system, make sure to exercise caution when working with the interfaces. If you are unsure about certain activities, such as port creation, ask a system administrator or someone knowledgeable to assist.

There is nothing wrong with asking for help and it is better than dealing with the consequences of an avoidable mistake.

## 3.2 Example 1—send invoices to an EDI partner

Assume we have an EDI partner (a customer) that wants to receive invoices in an EDI format (see Section 1.4 for more information on what EDI is). To achieve that, we will use the XML port created in Section 2.2 and add a new partner profile for the customer. Then we will use standard billing output type RD00 to create an IDoc.

Figure 3.1 presents a very simple diagram of such an interface. It is important to note that invoice creation, output, and the consequent IDoc creation are three completely separate processes. They could be configured to be performed automatically and seamlessly, but still each one of them presents a separate step with its own possible failure points. Keep this in mind when troubleshooting the IDoc interfaces. (Interface maintenance is covered in more detail in Chapter 5.)

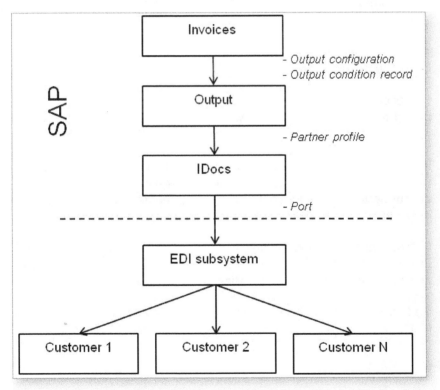

*Figure 3.1: Outbound EDI interface using output*

**EDI subsystem**

 Note that in the EDI communication, the IDocs are not sent directly to the partners (customers in this case) but need to be processed by a special application called "EDI subsystem" (see Figure 3.1) or "EDI translator."

This is needed because the SAP IDoc format is not the exact match for the EDI format (and there are different EDI standards on top of that). Also, it is not unusual for the EDI partners to have their own "flavors" of EDI implementation. As much as it should be standardized, alas, every partner loves adding their own finishing touches to it.

The SAP Process Orchestration (SAP PRO) solution can act as an EDI subsystem. Third-party software is also available to convert SAP IDoc format into various EDI formats.

## Output type configuration—Billing

Output configuration itself deserves a separate book, but since it is a vital part of the interface example, I will quickly review what configuration is typically needed.

In this example, we will use standard billing *output type* RD00. If you are using a different output type, or for some reason the standard output type in your system looks different (it is not a great idea to change standard output but it happens), you might need to make some adjustments.

Output configuration can be maintained in transaction SPRO, but we will use transaction NACE because it has everything we need in one place and can be used for many applications.

Go to transaction **NACE**, then scroll down the application list to V3 (Billing). Select the V3 line (it needs to be highlighted as in Figure 3.2).

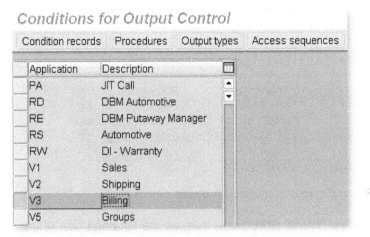

*Figure 3.2: Application types in Output Control*

Click OUTPUT TYPES to get a list of available output types (Figure 3.3). Scroll down to find RD00 output and double-click on it.

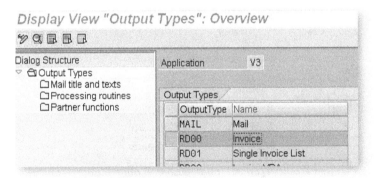

*Figure 3.3: Output types*

In the output type screen, on the left-hand side, we have the tree hierarchy DIALOG STRUCTURE. Double-click on the PROCESSING ROUTINES node (see Figure 3.3).

This takes us to a list of available mediums (i.e. output methods), corresponding processing programs, and routines (Figure 3.4). For this scenario, we must have an entry with medium EDI. Standard program for EDI output is RSNASTED, routine EDI_PROCESSING. It is possible to use a custom program, but I recommend sticking with the standard here.

43

| Output Type | RD00 | Invoice |
| Application | V3 | Billing |

| Processing routines | | | |
| Medium | Program | FORM routine | Fo |
| Print output | RVADIN01 | ENTRY | RV |
| Fax | RVADIN01 | ENTRY | RV |
| External send | SD_INVOICE_PRINT01 | ENTRY | SD |
| EDI | RSNASTED | EDI_PROCESSING | |
| Special function | RVALIN01 | ENTRY | |

*Figure 3.4: Processing routine assignment to output medium*

Now, in the same DIALOG STRUCTURE tree, on the left-hand side (Figure 3.3) double-click on the next node—PARTNER FUNCTIONS. There must be a partner function assigned to the EDI medium (see Figure 3.5). The Bill-to partner (BP) function works well in this scenario.

| Application | V3 | Billing |
| Output Type | RD00 | Invoice |

| Partner functions | | |
| Medium | Funct | Name |
| Print output | BP | Bill-to party |
| Fax | BP | Bill-to party |
| EDI | BP | Bill-to party |
| Distribution (ALE) | BP | Bill-to party |

*Figure 3.5: Partner functions for the output type*

Now we are ready for the next step.

## Define partner profile for customer

For this step, we will need the following information:

▶ Output type—in this example we will use standard billing output type RD00.

▶ Port—our test port is called XMLFILE (see Section 2.2)

▶ Customer account number—customer master data can be viewed in transactions XD03 or VD03, main database table is KNA1.

We will work with Bill-to partner in this example because this partner usually receives the invoices. The Bill-to partner function (BP) is also assigned to the RD00 output type in the standard output configuration reviewed above.

We can display the billing document in transaction **VF03**. Header partner information is located on the tab HEAD.PRTNRS (Figure 3.6).

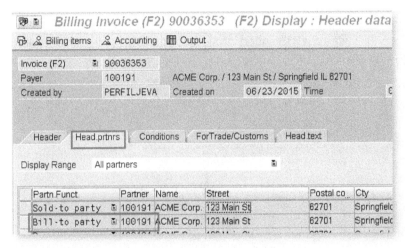

*Figure 3.6: Header partners in the billing document*

## Using other partners

 We can send the invoice IDoc to another header level partner, as long as the same partner function is maintained in both output type and partner profile. For example, if only the Sold-to function is available in the output and we configure partner profile for the Bill-to function, then obviously it is not going to work.

For EDI interfaces, the partner function must be the same in both the output and partner profile configurations.

To define a new partner profile, go to transaction **WE20**. Click on the CREATE (☐) icon, then enter the customer account number in the PARTNER NO field and KU (for Customer) in the PARTN. TYPE field (see Figure 3.7).

There are other required fields on the POST PROCESSING: PERMITTED AGENT tab. This always reminds me of James Bond and Austin Powers, but in this case the international man (or woman) of mystery is simply a person (or department) that is in charge of monitoring the interface. If there is an error in the IDoc processing, then a workflow task can be sent to that person (or group). For more information on this, see Section 5.2.

In this example, "agent" is an organizational unit, but for testing purposes you can also use type **US** (user) and enter your own (or your enemy's, hehe!) SAP user ID.

| Partner No. | 100191 | |
|---|---|---|
| Partn.Type | KU | Customer |

| Post processing: permitted agent | Classification | Telephony |
|---|---|---|

| Ty. | O | ☐ Organizational unit |
|---|---|---|
| Agent | 50010120 | EDI Department |
| Lang. | EN | English |

*Figure 3.7: Create new partner profile*

We don't need to do anything on the other tabs, but we do need to add an outbound parameter. To do that, click the icon CREATE OUTBOUND PARAMETER (🔳) underneath the OUTBOUND PARMTRS. table (Figure 3.8).

This will open the OUTBOUND PARAMETERS screen—see Figure 3.9. In this screen, we will add port, message type, output type, and other important information for our outbound interface.

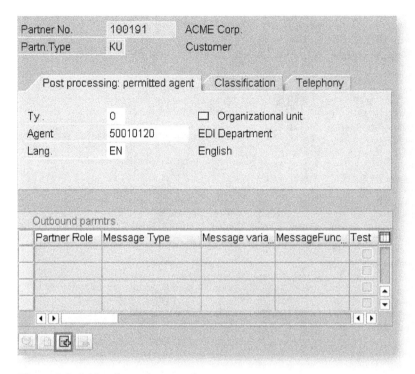

*Figure 3.8: Add outbound parameter*

Fill in the fields as follows:

▶ PARTNER ROLE—same as partner function in the output type configuration, in this example it is Bill-to (BP).

▶ MESSAGE TYPE—INVOIC.

▶ RECEIVER PORT—XMLFILE (see Section 2.2).

▶ BASIC TYPE—INVOIC02.

▶ Turn on TRANSFER IDOC IMMED. option (radio button).

47

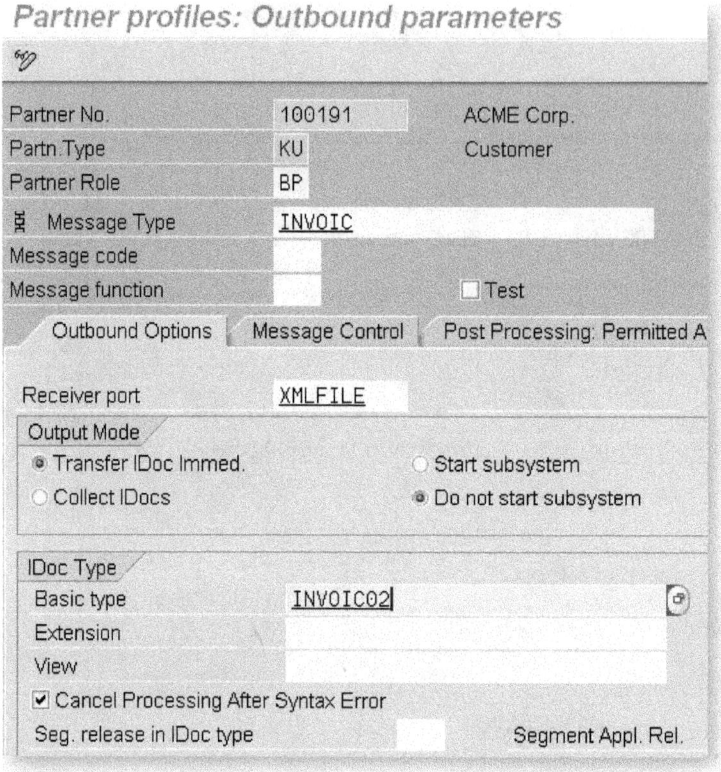

## Partner profiles: Outbound parameters

| Partner No. | 100191 | ACME Corp. |
| Partn.Type | KU | Customer |
| Partner Role | BP | |

Message Type    INVOIC

Message code

Message function    ☐ Test

| Outbound Options | Message Control | Post Processing: Permitted A |

Receiver port    XMLFILE

**Output Mode**
- ◉ Transfer IDoc Immed.          ○ Start subsystem
- ○ Collect IDocs                    ◉ Do not start subsystem

**IDoc Type**

| Basic type | INVOIC02 | |
| Extension | | |
| View | | |

☑ Cancel Processing After Syntax Error

Seg. release in IDoc type                    Segment Appl. Rel.

*Figure 3.9: Outbound options for INVOIC message type*

How do you know which message and IDoc type to use? Now, this is a million dollar question!

Unfortunately, there is no single comprehensive list of **all** of the IDocs and messages explaining their usage, but since this a mature technology, a lot of information is already available online.

For the EDI interfaces, SAP note **104606** provides message and IDoc type cross-references for the X12 standard (most common in North America). And at least some SAP message types (e.g. INVOIC) match EDIFACT standard (most common in Europe) names exactly. There is also an excellent SCN blog *Mapping IDocs to X12 Transactions and EDIFACT Messages* with a cross-reference of SAP message types vs. common EDI standards (see Appendix A, page 203).

The IDoc type is linked to the message type and there are usually not too many options. The rule of a thumb is to pick the latest IDoc type (i.e. the one with the largest number in the name) available, although there are some exceptions.

## Google is your friend

If you search in Google for "IDoc" followed by the document type or process (e.g. "IDoc EDI 810" or "IDoc for contract") you are very likely to find a helpful answer. Just make sure to use the standard SAP terminology, not industry jargon.

In the OUTPUT MODE area (Figure 3.9), we have two options: TRANSFER IDOC IMMEDIATELY and COLLECT IDOCS. What is the difference? If we select the "transfer immediately" option, then as soon as the IDoc is created it is also processed. In our example, an XML file is created immediately following the IDoc creation. If we choose the "collect" option, then IDoc is created but not processed until the special program is executed. For testing purposes, I always choose "transfer immediately" unless there is a specific need to do otherwise.

BASIC TYPE in this example is INVOIC02. (Basic type is the same thing as IDoc type, message, and IDoc type which were explained in Section 1.1.) If you click on the dropdown (or hit the F4 key) in this field you can view all the IDoc types available for the chosen message type.

## Basic type vs. IDoc type

Note that in Figure 3.9 the area labeled IDOC TYPE includes the fields labeled BASIC TYPE and EXTENSION. IDoc type was explained in Section 1.1, but how do other fields relate to it? "Basic type" simply means the standard SAP IDoc type and "Extension" is the custom IDoc extension (see Section 6.1). When using the standard IDoc type "as is" we only need to fill in BASIC TYPE field.

The next tab is MESSAGE CONTROL (Figure 3.10). In this tab, we link the partner profile and the output type. Click the ⊞ icon to add a new output type and fill in the fields as follows:

▶ APPLICATION—from the output configuration (Figure 3.2), the application type is V3 (if in doubt—use the dropdown).

▶ MESSAGE TYPE—this really should be labeled "output type" to avoid confusion with the previous screens. In this example, we use RD00 output type. Another type can be used as long as it is configured properly in transaction NACE.

▶ PROCESS CODE is SD09. How do I know that? To be honest, I just pick one value from the dropdown list that seems to make sense and usually it works. If it doesn't—I pick a different one and try again. If "third time the charm" does not happen, then it is time to call for reinforcements (see Appendix A).

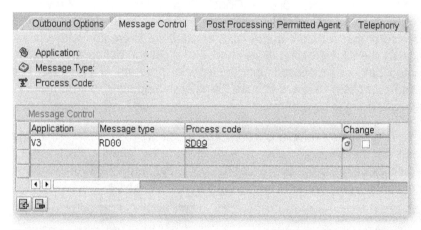

Figure 3.10: Message Control in the outbound parameter

This is all we need for now, save the profile.

## It's a boy, err, an IDoc!

Because output is processed separately from the document itself (see Figure 3.1), we actually don't need to create a new invoice and can easily add new output to an existing one. All we need is an invoice where the Bill-to partner is the same customer that we used in the partner profile.

You can create a new invoice, of course, but I recommend using an existing document for the first test, if possible. There is nothing more frustrating than running into some unrelated issues with invoice creation when you are just excited to see an IDoc already.

## How do I find an invoice?

To search for the invoices, use transaction VF05 or database table VBRK. If you need to search by Bill-to partner, then use table VBPA. There might also be custom reports or queries available in your system.

In this example, I will show how to add new EDI output to an existing invoice. Note that these steps are included for demonstration and testing purposes only. In the productive implementation, output should be triggered by the output condition records without any human intervention.

## Condition record maintenance

Output condition records for the billing documents are maintained in transaction VV31. Similar transactions exist for other documents (VV11 for sales orders, VV21 for deliveries, etc.). Transaction NACE can also be used, just click the CONDITION RECORDS button.

Note that unlike the output configuration itself, the condition records cannot be included in the transport request and have to be maintained manually in every SAP environment.

In transaction **VF02** enter the invoice number and hit the ⎡Enter⎦ key. On the next screen (Figure 3.11) go to the menu GOTO • HEADER • OUTPUT.

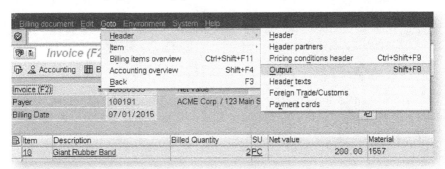

Figure 3.11: Output menu in VF02

This takes us to the CHANGE: OUTPUT screen. Enter output type RD00 in the first available line of OUTPUT table and hit the Enter key. If the output was configured correctly (and we have checked it), you should get something like what appears in Figure 3.12.

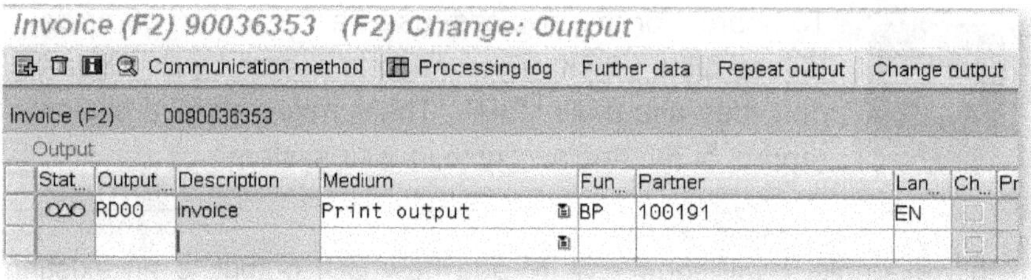

Invoice (F2) 90036353 (F2) Change: Output

🔲 🗑 🔳 🔍 Communication method 🔲 Processing log   Further data   Repeat output   Change output

| Invoice (F2) | 0090036353 | | | | | | | | | |
|---|---|---|---|---|---|---|---|---|---|---|
| Output | | | | | | | | | | |
| Stat. | Output | Description | Medium | | Fun. | Partner | | Lan. | Ch. | Pr |
| ∞ | RD00 | Invoice | Print output | 🔳 | BP | 100191 | | EN | | |
| | | | | 🔳 | | | | | | |

*Figure 3.12: New output added*

PARTNER and FUNCTION columns got filled in correctly with the Bill-to partner (Figure 3.12). But obviously, we don't need to print the output, we need an IDoc. No worries, we can easily put EDI in the MEDIUM column.

While we are at it, click the FURTHER DATA button to specify when the output should be processed. Since we are in a hurry to see the results, set the DISPATCH TIME to "Send immediately" (Figure 3.13).

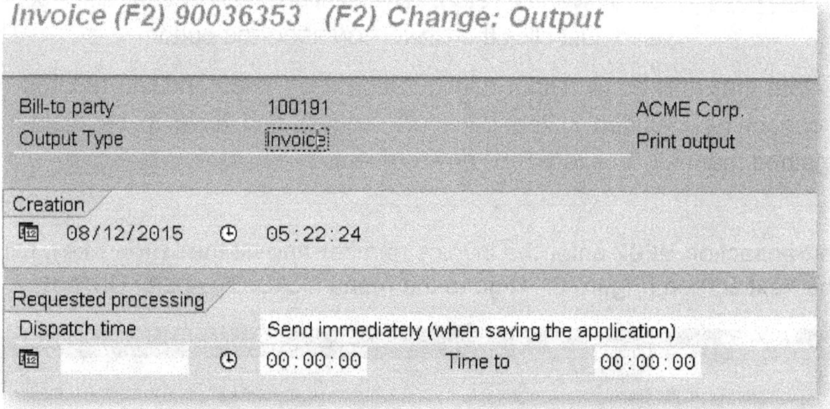

Invoice (F2) 90036353 (F2) Change: Output

| Bill-to party | 100191 | ACME Corp. |
|---|---|---|
| Output Type | Invoice | Print output |

Creation
📅 08/12/2015   🕐 05:22:24

Requested processing
Dispatch time          Send immediately (when saving the application)
📅                     🕐 00:00:00          Time to          00:00:00

*Figure 3.13: Further data settings*

Now go back to the CHANGE OUTPUT screen (Figure 3.14). Here is our output all ready to go with medium EDI and dispatch time 4 (i.e. "immediately").

*Invoice (F2) 90036353 (F2) Change: Output*

🔧 📋 🔖 🔍 Communication method  🎛 Processing log   Further data   Repeat output   Change output

Invoice (F2)    0090036353

Output

| Stat | Output | Description | Medium | Fun | Partner | Lan | Ch | Processing | Time | Date/Time |
|------|--------|-------------|--------|-----|---------|-----|----|-----------| -----|-----------|
| ◌◌◌ | RD00 | Invoice | EDI | BP | 100191 | EN | | | 00:00:00 | 4 |

*Figure 3.14: EDI output ready to be processed*

Finally, click the Save (🖫) icon and keep your fingers crossed. Seriously, keep them crossed for a few moments because it might take a while, especially for the first time, to get the output processed and IDoc created. To avoid disappointments, I usually stay in transaction VF02 and keep hitting Enter until I can get into the document. The invoice remains locked while output is processed, so when the invoice can be opened in change mode it means output processing has been completed.

Since we're already here, go to the OUTPUT screen again (menu GOTO • HEADER • OUTPUT) and, hopefully, you shall see your new output with the jolly green light next to it (Figure 3.15).

*Invoice (F2) 90036353 (F2) Change: Output*

🔧 📋 🔖 🔍 Communication method  🎛 Processing log   Further data   Repe

Invoice (F2)    0090036353

Output

| Stat | Output | Description | Medium | | Fun | Partner |
|------|--------|-------------|--------|---|-----|---------|
| ◌◌◌ | RD00 | Invoice | EDI | | BP | 100191 |

*Figure 3.15: Output processed successfully*

Yay! We can also click the PROCESSING LOG button to see the IDoc number in the log (Figure 3.16).

Output Processing analysis for proc. Billing Output

| Type | Message text |
|------|--------------|
| ⬚ | Object 0090036353 |
| ⬚ | Output type: Invoice |
| ⬚ | Processing log for program RSNASTED routine EDI_PROCESSING |
| ⬚ | IDoc '0000000000780745' was created and forwarded for transmission |
| ⬚ | IDoc '0000000000780745' written to file |

*Figure 3.16: Output processing log*

If you see a yellow light, it means output has not been processed yet. In this case, check if the immediate dispatch time is selected (click FURTHER DATA button).

If you see a red light, then uh-oh, we have a problem somewhere. Check the processing log for error messages. (See also Section 5.9 for the output troubleshooting tips.)

## Display IDoc and file

In transactions **VF02** and **VF03,** we have a neat button called SERVICES FOR OBJECT (💯 ⓘ), see Figure 3.17. If you click this icon and then choose RELATIONSHIPS from the dropdown, you will see the IDocs associated with the billing document. You can double-click on an IDoc to view it in detail.

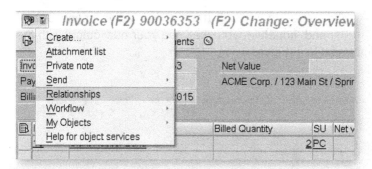

*Figure 3.17: Services for object—Relationships*

Of course, we can use transactions **WE02** or **WE05** (see Section 2.7) to display the IDoc as well. The IDoc number from the processing log can be entered on the selection screen in those transactions.

Here is our IDoc (Figure 3.18), everything looks nice and green. In the STATUS RECORDS node, we see status 03 with message "IDoc has been written in XML format in a file." Let's go check it out!

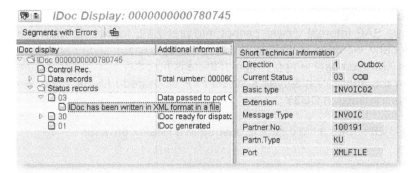

Figure 3.18: IDoc processed successfully

## Looking for the file name?

If you double-click on the message underneath status 03 it will also show the corresponding file name.

The file name can also be viewed in the port definition (transaction WE21), but if it is dynamic, then it might be difficult to figure out the exact file name for the particular IDoc.

To view the files on the application server, we can use transaction **AL11**.

In transaction **AL11,** double-click on the directory (the same one we used in the port definition in Section 2.2) and we should see the file there (Figure 3.19).

Directory: D:\usr\sap\I68\DVEBMGS00\data

| Useable | Viewed | Chang. | Length | File owner | File Name |
|---------|--------|--------|--------|------------|-----------|
| X | | | 7905 | SAPServi | idoc_document.xml |
| X | | | 191554 | SAPServi | stat.DAT |
| X | | | 685888 | SAPServi | stat.DAT100 |
| X | | | 684880 | SAPServi | stat.DAT101 |

Figure 3.19: XML file on the application server

If we double-click on the file, it will be displayed, but it will not look right because SAP internal viewer cannot interpret XML format. To view the file properly, we need to download it from the application server and open it in an XML-compatible application. If there is no other way to access the files on the application server, such as FTP or shared network drive, we can use transaction **CG3Y**.

Figure 3.20 shows a file example opened in a Firefox browser.

```
- <INVOIC02>
  - <IDOC BEGIN="1">
    - <EDI_DC40 SEGMENT="1">
        <TABNAM>EDI_DC40</TABNAM>
        <MANDT>850</MANDT>
        <DOCNUM>0000000000780745</DOCNUM>
        <DOCREL>740</DOCREL>
        <STATUS>30</STATUS>
        <DIRECT>1</DIRECT>
        <OUTMOD>2</OUTMOD>
        <IDOCTYP>INVOIC02</IDOCTYP>
        <MESTYP>INVOIC</MESTYP>
        <SNDPOR>SAPI68</SNDPOR>
        <SNDPRT>LS</SNDPRT>
```

*Figure 3.20: Invoice XML file example*

## 3.3   Example 2—send purchase orders to external system

Even though this example is for purchasing application, it is very similar to the previous one (Section 3.2).

In this scenario, we have an external system that needs information about the purchase orders created or changed in SAP. Just like in the previous scenario, we will use the output to generate an IDoc, but there are some differences in the partner profile and output setup. In this scenario, we will also use the logical system SKYNET that we created in Section 2.3.

Figure 3.21 shows a diagram of this interface. Just like in the previous example, it is important to note that every step (document creation or change, output, IDoc creation) is a separate process.

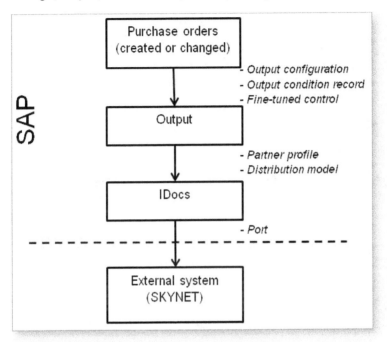

*Figure 3.21: Purchase order interface example*

## Output type configuration—Purchasing

In this example we will use the standard purchasing order output type NEU. Let's do a quick overview of its configuration.

Go to transaction **NACE**, select application EF for purchase orders (Figure 3.22), then click the OUTPUT TYPES button and double-click on NEU type.

**Conditions for Output Control**

| Condition records | Procedures | Output types | Ac |
|---|---|---|---|

| Application | Description | |
|---|---|---|
| CF | Error Control | ▲ |
| CV | Document Management | ▼ |
| E1 | Inbound Delivery | |
| EA | Purchasing RFQ | |
| EF | Purchase Order | |
| EL | Purch. SchAgrRelease | |

*Figure 3.22: Application list*

In the GENERAL DATA tab (Figure 3.23) for NEU output type, make sure that the MULTIPLE ISSUING checkbox is checked (we will need the output to be issued more than once in this example).

Also, there should be a program and routine assigned in the CHANGE OUTPUT section. This particular program ensures that a change flag is set when the output is created after making changes in the document.

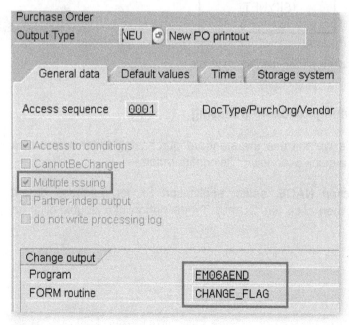

Purchase Order

Output Type    NEU   New PO printout

| General data | Default values | Time | Storage system |

Access sequence    0001    DocType/PurchOrg/Vendor

☑ Access to conditions
☐ CannotBeChanged
☑ Multiple issuing
☐ Partner-indep output
☐ do not write processing log

Change output

| Program | FM06AEND |
|---|---|
| FORM routine | CHANGE_FLAG |

*Figure 3.23: NEU output type configuration*

In the PROCESSING ROUTINES node (Figure 3.24), we need to have medium DISTRIBUTION (ALE) available. Standard program RSNASTED should work fine, as in the previous scenario. The routine name for the ALE medium is ALE_PROCESSING.

| Dialog Structure | Output Type | NEU | New PO printout |
|---|---|---|---|
| ▽ ☐ Output Types | Application | EF | Purchase Order |
| ☐ Mail title and texts | | | |
| ☐ Processing routines | | | |
| ☐ Partner functions | | | |

Processing routines

| Medium | | Program | FORM routine | F |
|---|---|---|---|---|
| Print output | 🔲 | ZMM_FM06P | ENTRY_NEU | |
| Fax | 🔲 | SAPFM06P | ENTRY_NEU | M |
| External send | 🔲 | SAPFM06P | ENTRY_NEU | M |
| EDI | 🔲 | RSNASTED | EDI_PROCESSING | |
| Simple Mail | 🔲 | SAPFM06P | ENTRY_NEU | M |
| Distribution (ALE) | 🔲 | RSNASTED | ALE_PROCESSING | |
| | 🔲 | | | |

*Figure 3.24: NEU output – Processing routine assignment*

## ALE vs. EDI

In the previous scenario we used medium EDI, but in this scenario we are using ALE. Why? Truth is—whether we use ALE or EDI, we will end up with the same IDoc as a result. The difference is in the partner settings.

In the previous scenario, we had one customer as a partner. In this scenario, our partner is a logical system. If we were sending purchase orders to an EDI partner (vendor) then we would also use the EDI medium and vendor (VN) type partner profile. But we have to use the ALE medium with the logical system (LS) partner type. (Hmm, maybe we just found what the actual difference between EDI and ALE is.)

Under the PARTNER FUNCTIONS node (Figure 3.25), we should have medium DISTRIBUTION (ALE) assigned to VN (Vendor) function. In this case, the partner function is only relevant for the output proposal.

| Dialog Structure | Application | EF |
| --- | --- | --- |
| ▽ ☐ Output Types | Output Type | NEU |
| ☐ Mail title and texts | | |
| ☐ Processing routines | | |
| ☐ Partner functions | | |

Partner functions

| Medium | Funct | Name |
| --- | --- | --- |
| Distribution (ALE) ▣ | VN | Vendor |
| ▣ | | |

*Figure 3.25: NEU output – partner functions*

## Partner function significance

This part frequently causes confusion. In the previous EDI example (Section 3.2), the same partner function was set up in the output, in the document, and in the partner profile. But in this case, the partner function exists only in the document and output type. There is no partner function for the logical system.

The output determination configuration relies on the partner function, so we do need to maintain a valid function (VN in this example) in the output type.

When the same partner function is found in the document (purchase order in this example), it is used to propose the output according to the configuration. It is not possible to get any output without a valid partner function in both the document and the configuration (it is a vital link between the two).

When we use the ALE medium instead of EDI, the partner function is not taken into consideration when searching for the partner profile. Instead, the logical system (LS) profile is used to create an IDoc from the output.

## Define partner profile for logical system

The steps here are similar to the previous scenario except instead of the KU (customer) profile type we will use the LS (logical system) type.

In transaction **WE20,** click the CREATE icon (▢) and fill in the fields (Figure 3.26):

- ▶ PARTNER NO—SKYNET (logical system created in Section 2.3)
- ▶ PARTN.TYPE—LS
- ▶ AGENT—does not matter at this point, you can enter your SAP user ID there, for example.

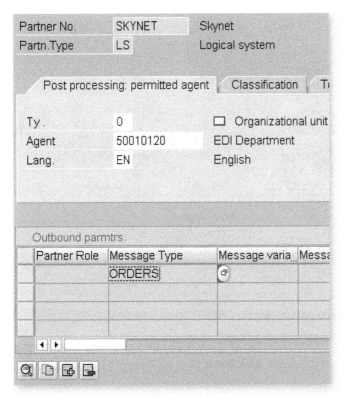

*Figure 3.26: New partner profile for logical system*

In this example, we need to add two outbound message types to the profile: one for the purchase order creation (ORDERS) and one for the changes (ORDCHG). Let's start with the first one.

Click the CREATE OUTBOUND PARAMETER icon (🗐) to add a new message type.

On the OUTBOUND PARAMETERS screen (Figure 3.27), fill in the fields on the OUTBOUND OPTIONS tab:

▶ MESSAGE TYPE—ORDERS

▶ PORT—XMLFILE (same in all examples)

▶ BASIC TYPE—ORDERS05

▶ Turn on TRANSFER IDOC IMMED. option (radio button)

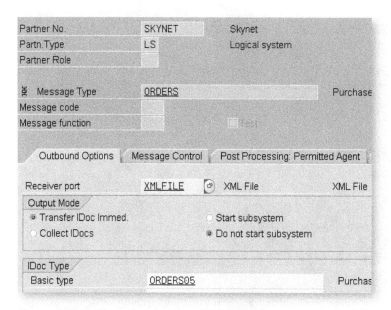

*Figure 3.27: Outbound parameters for ORDERS message type*

Open the MESSAGE CONTROL tab (Figure 3.28) and click the INSERT ROW (⊞) icon, then fill in the fields as follows:

▶ APPLICATION—EF

▶ MESSAGE TYPE—NEU

▶ PROCESS CODE—ME10

Save the changes and go back to the PARTNER PROFILE screen (Figure 3.26).

| Outbound Options | Message Control | Post Processing: Permitted Agent | Teler |

🐚 Application:      EF : Purchase Order
◇ Message Type:      NEU : New PO printout
🎇 Process Code:      ME10 : ORDERS: Purchase order

Message Control

| Application | Message type | Process code | | Change |
|---|---|---|---|---|
| EF | NEU | ME10 | ☞ | ☐ |
| | | | | |
| | | | | |

*Figure 3.28: Message Control settings for ORDERS message type*

Since the second message type (ORDCHG) has similar settings, we can copy the entry we just created. Select the line with the ORDERS message type and click COPY (Figure 3.29). The warning message "Outbound parameters are copied without Message Control" displays. No big deal, we can add it.

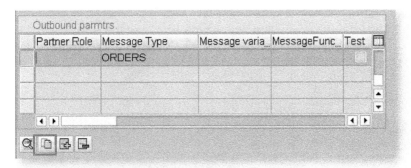

| Partner Role | Message Type | Message varia.. | MessageFunc.. | Test | ⬚ |
|---|---|---|---|---|---|
| | ORDERS | | | ☐ | |
| | | | | | |
| | | | | | |

*Figure 3.29: Copy existing message type*

In the OUTBOUND OPTIONS tab, we should now have the same exact information as for the ORDERS message type. Simply replace ORDERS with ORDCHG in the MESSAGE TYPE field (Figure 3.30).

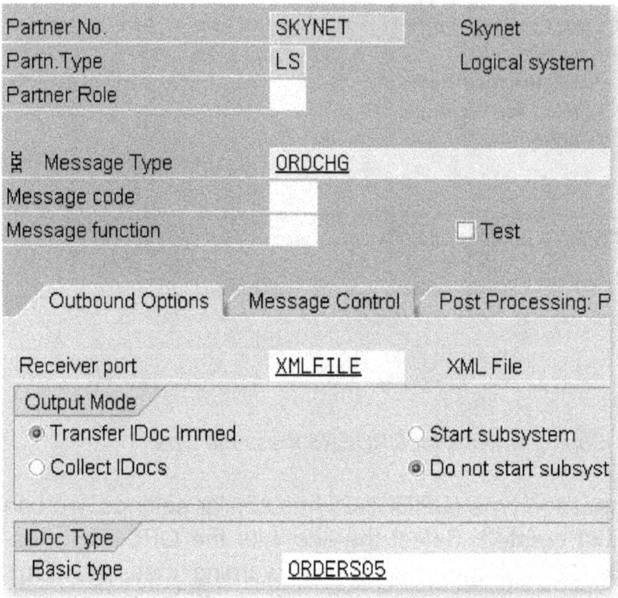

| Partner No. | SKYNET | Skynet |
|---|---|---|
| Partn.Type | LS | Logical system |
| Partner Role | | |

| Message Type | ORDCHG | |
|---|---|---|
| Message code | | |
| Message function | | ☐ Test |

| Outbound Options | Message Control | Post Processing: P |
|---|---|---|

Receiver port     XMLFILE     XML File

Output Mode
- ● Transfer IDoc Immed.     ○ Start subsystem
- ○ Collect IDocs     ● Do not start subsyst

IDoc Type
Basic type     ORDERS05

*Figure 3.30: Outbound options for ORDCHG message*

MESSAGE CONTROL tab (Figure 3.31) will also look similar (see Figure 3.28). Keep application EF and output type NEU, but the PROCESS CODE in this case is ME11 and (important!) we also need to check the CHANGE checkbox.

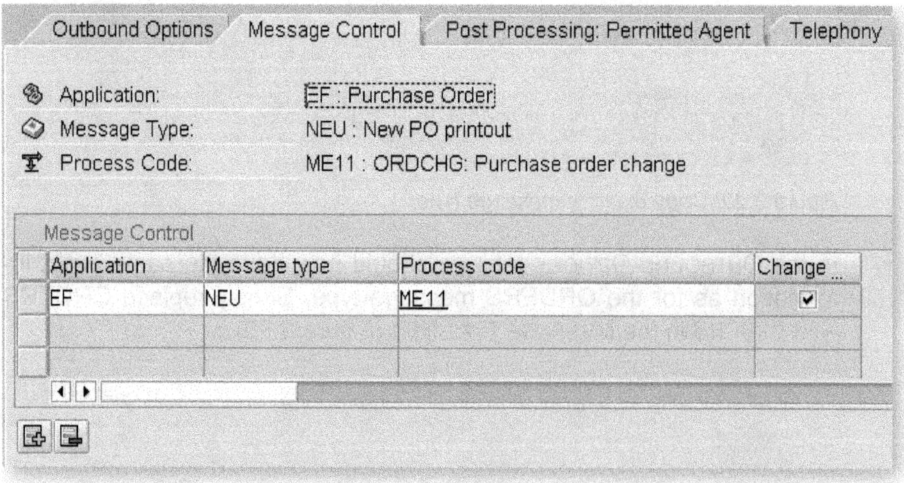

| Outbound Options | Message Control | Post Processing: Permitted Agent | Telephony |
|---|---|---|---|

Application:     EF : Purchase Order
Message Type:     NEU : New PO printout
Process Code:     ME11 : ORDCHG: Purchase order change

Message Control

| Application | Message type | Process code | Change |
|---|---|---|---|
| EF | NEU | ME11 | ☑ |
| | | | |
| | | | |

*Figure 3.31: Message Control settings for ORDCHG message type*

Once you are done with the profile, save the changes.

## Change tracking—additional configuration

For the purchasing documents, an additional configuration is available to fine tune the change tracking.

If you are using standard output NEU (as in this example), then this configuration should already be completed. But if you are using a custom output type or need to specify different fields to track, you might have to make some changes in it. This configuration is transportable; prompt for a transport request will appear when saving.

An output type needs to be added to the "Fine-Tuned Control" field in transaction **OMQN**. We can also use transaction SPRO with the following path: MATERIALS MANAGEMENT • PURCHASING • MESSAGES • OUTPUT CONTROL • MESSAGE TYPES • DEFINE MESSAGE TYPE FOR PURCHASE ORDER • FINE-TUNED CONTROL: PURCHASE ORDER.

Make sure an entry exists for the output type (NEU in this example) and operation 2 (Change), see Figure 3.32.

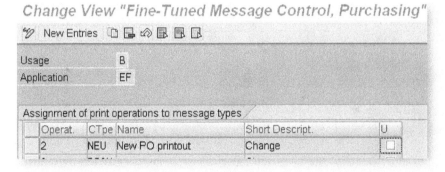

*Figure 3.32: Transaction OMQN*

Specific fields to track can be defined in transaction **OMFS** (SPRO path: MATERIALS MANAGEMENT • PURCHASING • MESSAGES • FIELDS RELEVANT TO PRINTOUTS OF CHANGES). Here we see the database table and field names (see Figure 3.33). To track the field changes in the purchase order, check the checkbox in column P ("Change Print Relevant Purchase Order") next to the corresponding field name.

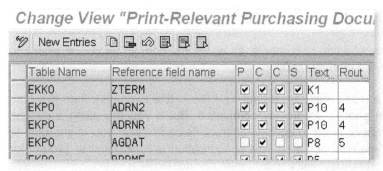

| Table Name | Reference field name | P | C | C | S | Text | Rout |
|---|---|---|---|---|---|---|---|
| EKKO | ZTERM | ✔ | ✔ | ✔ | ✔ | K1 | |
| EKPO | ADRN2 | ✔ | ✔ | ✔ | ✔ | P10 | 4 |
| EKPO | ADRNR | ✔ | ✔ | ✔ | ✔ | P10 | 4 |
| EKPO | AGDAT | ☐ | ✔ | ☐ | ☐ | P8 | 5 |
| EKPO | DDDME | ✔ | ✔ | ✔ | ✔ | DE | |

*Figure 3.33: Transaction OMFS*

### Finding technical field names

To find the database table and field name for a field in any transaction click the `F1` (Help) key while the cursor is in that field. In the Help pop-up, click on the TECHNICAL DETAIL icon (📊). The main database tables for the purchasing documents are: EKKO (header), EKPO (line items), and EKET (schedule lines).

### Mind the impact

Keep in mind that the configuration in transaction OMFS applies to all the purchase order output, not just to one particular output type. If your scenario requires different or more granular change tracking, you might need to develop a custom ABAP program.

## Distribution model for a purchase order

In this scenario, we have an outbound interface with an external system. In an SAP system, we use the logical system SKYNET (created in Section 2.3) to represent this external system.

Before we can begin, we need to find what logical system is assigned to the current SAP client. This information is available in transaction **SCC4** (double-click on the client number), field LOGICAL SYSTEM (Figure 3.34). Take a note of this value, we will need it.

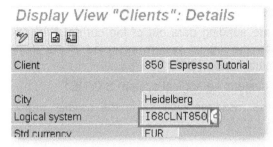

*Figure 3.34: Logical system for the current client*

To create a distribution model, go to the transaction **BD64**. This transaction opens in display mode by default, click the 🖉 button to switch to change mode (Figure 3.35).

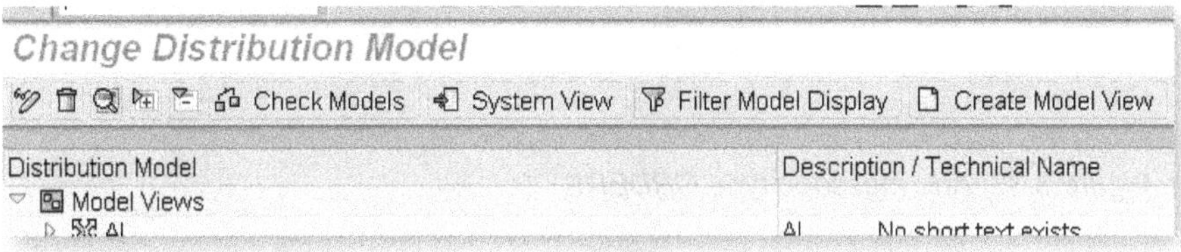

### Change Distribution Model

🖉 🗑 🔍 📋 📑 🔏 Check Models  🔷 System View  🦅 Filter Model Display  🗋 Create Model View

| Distribution Model | Description / Technical Name |
|---|---|
| ▽ 🔳 Model Views | |
| ▷ 🔧 AI | AI    No short text exists |

*Figure 3.35: Distribution model*

First, we need to create a model view, as was mentioned in Section 2.3. To keep it simple, for the model view, we will use the same name as the logical system (SKYNET).

Click the CREATE MODEL VIEW button and fill in TECHNICAL NAME and DE-SCRIPTION. Start/end dates are irrelevant in this example, so leave them as is.

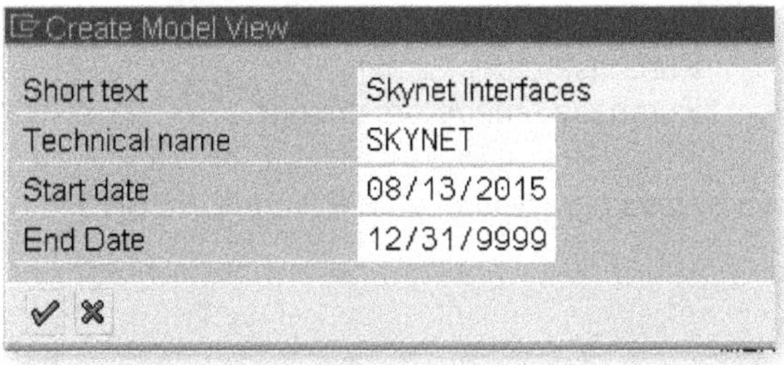

### Create Model View

| Short text | Skynet Interfaces |
|---|---|
| Technical name | SKYNET |
| Start date | 08/13/2015 |
| End Date | 12/31/9999 |

✔ ✖

*Figure 3.36: Create model view*

67

Now we can add message types to this model view by clicking ADD MES-SAGE TYPE. In the pop-up screen, enter the following fields (Figure 3.37):

▶ MODEL VIEW—the one we have just created (SKYNET)

▶ SENDER—since we are sending data out of the current SAP cli-ent, we need to enter the logical system assigned to the client (the one we got from transaction SCC4)

▶ RECEIVER—external system, i.e. logical system SKYNET

▶ MESSAGE TYPE—same message type as in the partner profile (ORDERS)

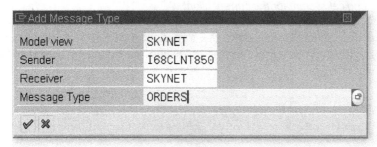

*Figure 3.37: Add message type ORDERS*

Repeat this step to add the ORDCHG message type. The end result should look similar to what appears in Figure 3.38.

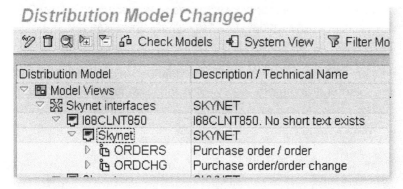

*Figure 3.38: Distribution model with message types ORDERS and ORDCHG*

Save it.

## Purchase order creation

In this example, we need to make sure that IDoc is generated when we create the purchase order and when we change the purchase order.

We will start with creating a new purchase order in transaction **ME21N**. After filling in all the required fields (this will vary based on your system's configuration), we can add output.

In the previous example, we used a menu to get to the output screen, but in this transaction, we need to use the MESSAGES button (Figure 3.39). It will take us to the same screen though (compare to Figure 3.12).

| 🗎 | *Create Purchase Order* | | | | | | | | |

| ocument Overview On | 🗋 🕏 Hold | Park 🖧 | 🗗 Print Preview | Messages | 🖪 🗗 Persi |

| 📄 NB Standard PO | 🗎 | Vendor | 100248 Wayne Enterprises |
| Header |

| 🖪 | S | Itm | A | I | Material | Short Text | PO Quantity | OUr |
|---|---|---|---|---|---|---|---|---|
| | | 10 | | | TI-MODULE | Batmobile Module Assembly | 2 | EA |

*Figure 3.39: Create purchase order—ME21N*

If the output condition records have been maintained, you might already see the output type (NEU in this case) in this screen. If not, we can add it manually using the 🖪 icon. In this scenario, we need to use "Distribution (ALE)" medium (Figure 3.40).

| | *Create Pur. Order :: Output* | | | | | |

| 🖪 🗎 🖪 🔍 Communication method | 🖽 Processing log | Further data | Repeat output |

| Pur. Order......... |
| Output |

| | Stat | Output | Description | Medium | | Fun | Partner | Lan | C |
|---|---|---|---|---|---|---|---|---|---|
| | ○○○ | NEU | New PO printo... | A Distribution (ALE) 🗎 | | VN | 100248 | EN | |
| | | | | | 🗎 | | | | |

*Figure 3.40: Purchase order—NEU output*

Click the FURTHER DATA button and choose the SEND IMMEDIATELY option in DISPATCH TIME field (Figure 3.41).

## Create Pur. Order :: Output

| | | |
|---|---|---|
| Vendor | 100248 | Wayne Enterpi |
| Output Type | New PO printout | Distribution (A |

Creation
🖻 09/17/2015 🕓 04:55:32

Requested processing
Dispatch time    | 4 Send immediately (when saving the application)
🖻               | 🕓 00:00:00    Time to    00:00:00

*Figure 3.41: NEU output—dispatch time*

Click the SAVE icon and—abracadabra! When we get back into the purchase order (after waiting for a few seconds to allow the system to process output) and click the MESSAGES button again, we can see the green light in the STATUS column (Figure 3.42) and IDoc information in the processing log (Figure 3.43).

## Change Pur. Order :: Output

🖻 🗑 🖬 🔍 Communication method   ⊞ Processing log   Further data   R

Pur. Order.......... 4500017269

Output

| Stat. | Output | Description | Medium | | Fun. | Partner |
|---|---|---|---|---|---|---|
| COO | NEU | New PO printo... | A Distribution (A... | 🖺 | VN | 100248 |
| | | | | 🖺 | | |

*Figure 3.42: NEU output processed successfully*

Output Processing analysis for proc. Purchase Order

| Type | Message text |
|---|---|
| ▢ | Object 4500017269 |
| ▢ | Output type: New PO printout |
| ▢ | Processing log for program RSNASTED routine ALE_PROCESSING |
| ▢ | IDoc '0000000000785745' was created and forwarded for transmission |
| ▢ | IDoc '0000000000785745' written to file |

*Figure 3.43: Processing log for NEU output*

As usual, to display the IDoc, we can use transaction WE02 or WE05 (Figure 3.44).

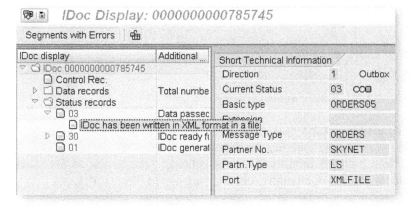

Figure 3.44: ORDERS IDoc for purchase order

## Purchase order change

Now we can make a change in the same purchase order and see what happens. Keep in mind that only the relevant fields (as defined in transaction OMFS) will trigger an output when changed.

### Time for the output condition records

 If you have not done so already, at this point I recommend maintaining at least one output condition record for the output type (NEU in this example) in transaction **MN04**. To ensure that you get any output for testing purposes, use the least restrictive key, e.g. Purchase Organization.

Maintaining output condition records allows the output to be proposed automatically. This is a better option for testing the output of changes. If you run into any issues with the output, see Section 5.9 for troubleshooting tips.

Go to transaction **ME22N**. Change the PO QUANTITY field and then click MESSAGES button (Figure 3.45).

Standard PO 4500017269 Created by Jelena PERFILJEVA

| ent Overview On | 🗋 🦅 🔁 🗗 | 🗇 Print Preview | Messages | 🖩 🔁 Personal Setting |
|---|---|---|---|---|

| Standard PO | 🖹 4500017269 | Vendor | 100248 Wayne Enterprises |
|---|---|---|---|

| Itm | A | I | Material | Short Text | PO Quantity | OUn | C | Deliv. [ |
|---|---|---|---|---|---|---|---|---|
| 10 | | | TI-MODULE | Batmobile Module Assembly | 3 | EA | D | 09/17 |

*Figure 3.45: Making changes in the purchase order*

If the condition records have been maintained correctly, then we should see the NEU output already proposed on the OUTPUT screen (Figure 3.46). Note that this time the CHANGE indicator (check box) is set. This indicator is set by the change program assigned to the output type.

If you need to add another NEU output manually, then the simplest way is to select an existing output line and click REPEAT OUTPUT button.

Change Pur. Order :: Output

| 🗐 🗂 🖩 🔍 Communication method | 🖽 Processing log | Further data | Repeat output | C |
|---|---|---|---|---|

Pur. Order......... 4500017269

Output

| Stat | Output | Description | Medium | | Fun | Partner | Lan | Change | F |
|---|---|---|---|---|---|---|---|---|---|
| ○∆○ | NEU | New PO printou | Distribution (ALE) 🖹 | | VN | 100248 | EN | ☑ | |
| ○○□ | NEU | New PO printo | Distribution (ALE) 🖹 | | VN | 100248 | EN | ☐ | [ |

*Figure 3.46: Purchase order output after a change*

Save the order again and a few seconds later we should see the output status turn green.

As usual, we can find the IDoc number in the log (PROCESSING LOG button) and then view the IDoc in transaction WE02 or WE05. Note that this time the IDoc has message type ORDCHG (Figure 3.47).

Figure 3.48 shows a fragment of the XML file that was created from the IDoc. Segment EDI_DC40 represents the IDoc control record.

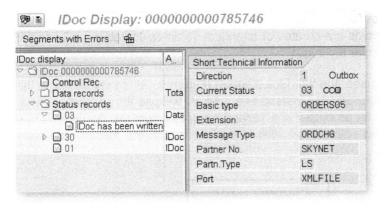

Figure 3.47: ORDCHG Idoc

```
- <ORDERS05>
  - <IDOC BEGIN="1">
    - <EDI_DC40 SEGMENT="1">
        <TABNAM>EDI_DC40</TABNAM>
        <MANDT>850</MANDT>
        <DOCNUM>0000000000785746</DOCNUM>
        <DOCREL>740</DOCREL>
        <STATUS>30</STATUS>
        <DIRECT>1</DIRECT>
        <OUTMOD>2</OUTMOD>
        <IDOCTYP>ORDERS05</IDOCTYP>
        <MESTYP>ORDCHG</MESTYP>
        <SNDPOR>SAPI68</SNDPOR>
        <SNDPRT>LS</SNDPRT>
        <SNDPRN>I68CLNT850</SNDPRN>
        <RCVPOR>XMLFILE</RCVPOR>
        <RCVPRT>LS</RCVPRT>
        <RCVPRN>SKYNET</RCVPRN>
```

Figure 3.48: XML file for ORDCHG IDoc

## 3.4    Example 3—send master data to an external system

In this example, we need to create an interface to send the customer master data from an SAP system to another system. The other system will be represented in SAP by the same logical system SKYNET as in the previous scenario.

73

For this interface, we will need to create an IDoc whenever the customer master records are created or changed. To achieve that, we will use the *change pointer* technique.

As you can see, the interface diagram (Figure 3.49) is very similar to the previous interface, but instead of output we will use the change pointers. Note that just as output is a separate process from the document creation, change pointers are also independent from the master data entry step.

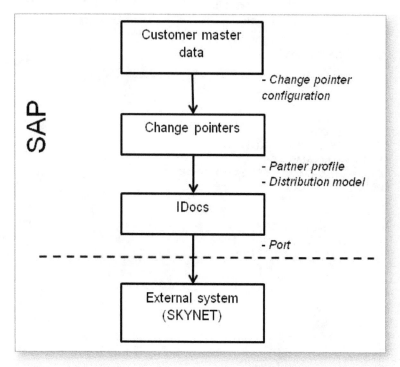

*Figure 3.49: Customer master data interface example*

As you might already know, many changes in SAP (including master data) are tracked using *change documents*. In a nutshell, change documents are just the records in the special database tables: CDHDR (header) and CDPOS (details). Based on the change documents, the additional records called "change pointers" are created. Change pointers are also simply the records in the database tables (table names start with "BDCP").

When special program **RBDMIDOC** (or transaction **BD21**) is executed, it reads those records and creates the IDocs accordingly. And to make sure that the same change is not sent out more than once, the change pointer records are marked as processed. If you just had a question as to why change pointers are needed on top of the change documents— that's the answer. Change documents track all the changes, but change pointers: (a) track only what is relevant to the IDoc interfaces and (b) are used to mark the changes already sent. Are you with me so far? Good!

There are some additional activities required to start using change pointers, let's go over them.

### Clean-up on aisle 5!

 The change pointer tables can become very large very fast. Make sure to read **SAP Note 513454** "REP: High-performance operation with change pointers" and schedule report RBDCPCLR (transaction BD22) to clean up the processed records periodically.

Note that only processed records can be "cleaned up". It is important to prevent accumulation of change pointer data that cannot or should not be processed.

## Change pointer activation

Naturally, not every company running SAP requires change pointers and it would be a waste to generate all those records unnecessarily.

That is why change pointers need to be activated before we can use them and can be deactivated when not in use. There are three activation levels:

- ▶ at the SAP client level ("generally"),
- ▶ at the message type level,
- ▶ at the field level.

Transaction **BD61** enables the change pointers at the client level. This must be the silliest transaction in SAP: all it has is one single checkbox (Figure 3.50). However, it does have quite an impact! When the checkbox is checked, the change pointers are active in the current SAP client. Note that this is a transportable configuration, so you are prompted for a transport when saving changes.

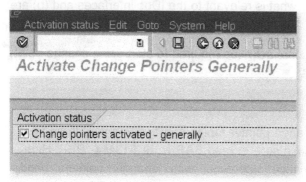

*Figure 3.50: Transaction BD61*

To enable change pointers for the specific message type, go to transaction **BD50**. Each message type corresponds to a certain data type. The DEBMAS message type is used for the customer master data (Figure 3.51).

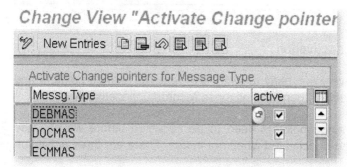

*Figure 3.51: Activate change pointers for DEBMAS message*

Keep in mind that this change pointer configuration affects the whole message type, not just one particular interface, so make sure not to step on anyone's toes when making changes.

In transaction **BD52,** we can specify which fields should trigger the change pointer creation. First, we need to specify the corresponding message type (all change pointers relate to the specific message types), then remove or add the specific fields (Figure 3.52).

Note that the single message type may include fields from multiple database tables.

| Change View "Change document items for r | | |
|---|---|---|
| ✌ New Entries ⬚ ⬚ ⬚ ⬚ ⬚ ⬚ | | |
| Message Type | DEBMAS | |

Change document items for message type

| Object | Table Name | Field Name | |
|---|---|---|---|
| DEBI | KNA1 | BBSNR | ⬚ |
| DEBI | KNA1 | BEGRU | |
| DEBI | KNA1 | BRAN1 | |
| DEBI | KNA1 | BRAN2 | |

*Figure 3.52: Configure fields relevant for change tracking*

## Update partner profile

We have already created a partner profile for the logical system SKYNET in the previous scenario (see Section 3.3).

In transaction **WE20,** locate the partner profile for logical system SKYNET (see Figure 3.26). Click the CREATE OUTBOUND PARAMETER icon (⬚) to add a new message type (Figure 3.53). Fill in the fields as follows:

- ▶ MESSAGE TYPE— DEBMAS
- ▶ PORT—XMLFILE (same in all examples)
- ▶ BASIC TYPE— DEBMAS07
- ▶ Turn on TRANSFER IDOC IMMED. option (radio button)

In this example, I chose IDoc type DEBMAS07 because it is the latest version available. You can use a different IDoc type based on what is available in your system and your specific requirements.

**Partner profile generation**

It is also possible to generate the partner profiles from the distribution model. See Section 2.3 for more information on this.

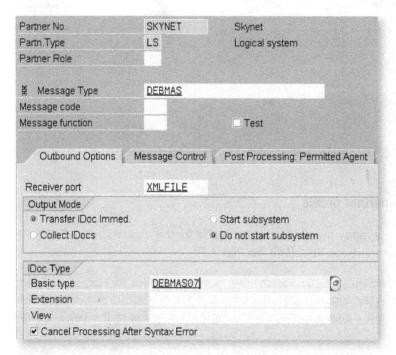

*Figure 3.53: Outbound parameters for DEBMAS message type*

We are not using Message Control or any special functions in this scenario, so save the profile change.

## Distribution model for customer master data

We have already created a logical system in Section 2.3 and added a model view while working on the previous scenario (see Section 3.3). At this point, all we need is to add another message type to the same model view.

In transaction **BD64,** select the SKYNET model view (see Figure 3.36) and click the ADD MESSAGE TYPE button. Fill in the fields as follows (Figure 3.54):

- ▶ MODEL VIEW—SKYNET
- ▶ SENDER—logical system assigned to the current (see transaction SCC4)
- ▶ RECEIVER—external system, i.e. logical system SKYNET
- ▶ MESSAGE TYPE—same message type as in the partner profile (DEBMAS)

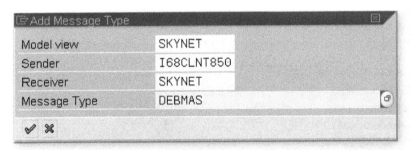

*Figure 3.54: Add DEBMAS message type*

Save the changes.

## Create a customer master record

Now that we have completed all the IDoc-related configuration, it's time to create a new customer record, then change it and see what happens.

Customer master records can be created in transaction **XD01** or **VD01** (the last one does not include the company code view). Both transactions would work for testing purposes, but note that the screens and steps may vary depending on the system configuration.

If you can create a new customer with a reference to an existing one (CUSTOMER field in REFERENCE section), it will save time on the data entry (Figure 3.55). Otherwise, select a value for ACCOUNT GROUP ("Sold-to party" in this example) and click ✅ to proceed.

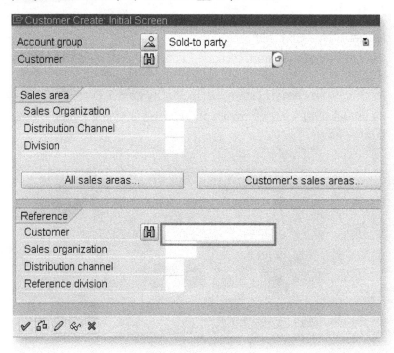

*Figure 3.55: Create customer, initial screen*

For this test, we only need to fill in the required fields to be able to save the record (Figure 3.56).

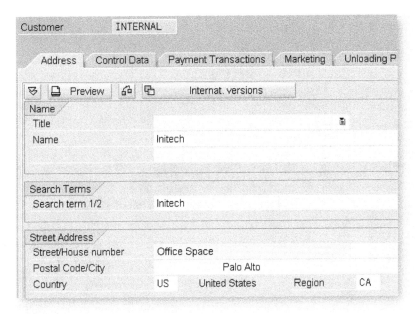

*Figure 3.56: New customer account*

Upon saving, we should get a confirmation message with the new customer account number (Figure 3.57).

*Figure 3.57: Customer account created—confirmation*

## Process change pointers

At this point, the change document and change pointer records should already be generated. To process them and create an IDoc, we can use transaction **BD21** (Figure 3.58). All we need to enter is message type DEBMAS, then execute the transaction.

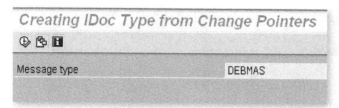

Figure 3.58: Create IDoc from change pointers

**Report vs. transaction**

Transaction BD21 is the same as the RBDMIDOC report. This transaction can be used for testing, but in a productive environment the change pointers are usually processed by the report running in a background job.

When I did that in a test system, the first message I got was: "1 master IDocs set up for message type DEBMAS". This is exactly what I expected—one customer was created and one IDoc should be generated. But why did it say "master IDoc"?

Funny story. In the master data distribution with a change pointer scenario, SAP first creates what is called *the master IDoc*. Despite the name, it is **not** the actual IDoc (meaning that we cannot see it in WE02/WE05) but rather a template that is used to create the *communication IDoc* (which **is** the actual IDoc) for each interface where the corresponding data needs to be distributed.

The next message I saw was "15 communication IDoc(s) generated for message type DEBMAS". What the deuce?! I don't need 15 IDocs! What have I done?!

Transaction WE02 gleefully presented me the consequence of my irresponsible actions and indeed there were 15 IDocs – only one of which had the logical system SKYNET as a recipient. Judging by the control records, the other 14 IDocs were meant for some other logical systems and, to my relief, they were not sent anywhere due to a communication error.

What happened here? For this test, I was using an IDES system kindly provided by the publisher. Unbeknownst to me (i.e. I didn't bother checking), other distribution models existed in the same system for other logical systems that also "wanted" the DEBMAS message for the customer master records. That is why when I ran the program for the message type, it generated so many IDocs for just one change—there were 15 recipients set up to receive the same data.

This could be either a desired effect or a problem. If only certain records need to be sent to the specific logical system, we will need to use filters in the distribution model (see Section 2.6) or a more complex customization.

Figure 3.59 shows the IDoc that was created as a result of the change pointer processing. Since we filled in only basic information in the customer master, there are only two data segments. Note that the segment E1KNA1M contains the field MSGFN (Function) with the code 009, which means that this IDoc represents a newly created customer master record.

The possible values for this field and other information can be viewed in transaction **WE60** (see Section 1.3).

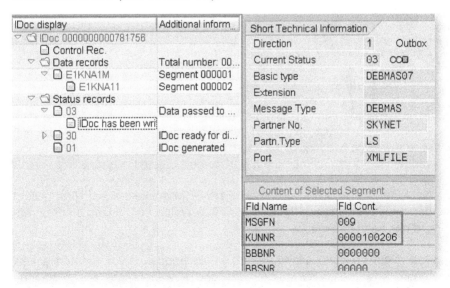

*Figure 3.59: IDoc for new customer account*

## Wash, rinse, repeat

Now we need to change the customer master record to make sure it also triggers IDoc creation. To make this change, use the transaction **XD02** or **VD02** (there is no Company Code view in VD02). No need to get super creative here, a simple street address change (Figure 3.60) will do for this test.

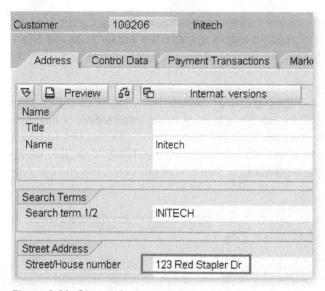

*Figure 3.60: Change in the customer master record*

Save the change.

To process the change pointers, follow the same steps as before (see Figure 3.58): transaction **BD21**, enter message type DEBMAS, execute, read the same two messages about the master and communication IDocs, yada-yada-yada, and then the new IDoc gets created (Figure 3.61).

Note that this time in the segment E1KNA1M the field MSGFN (Function) has a different value: 004 instead of 009. Value 004 means that the record has been changed.

You might be curious about what would happen if you created a new record and then very quickly changed it without processing change pointers in between. Would you get two IDocs?

| IDoc display | Additional information | Short Technical Information | | |
|---|---|---|---|---|
| ▽ ▭ IDoc 0000000000781771 | | Direction | 1 | Outbox |
| ▭ Control Rec. | | | | |
| ▽ ▭ Data records | Total number: 000002 | Current Status | 03 | ☐☐☐ |
| ▽ ▭ E1KNA1M | Segment 000001 | Basic type | DEBMAS07 | |
| ▭ E1KNA11 | Segment 000002 | Extension | | |
| ▽ ▭ Status records | | Message Type | DEBMAS | |
| ▽ ▭ 03 | Data passed to port O | Partner No. | SKYNET | |
| ▭ IDoc has been writ | | Partn.Type | LS | |
| ▷ ▭ 30 | IDoc ready for dispatcl | Port | XMLFILE | |
| ▭ 01 | IDoc generated | | | |

| Content of Selected Segment | |
|---|---|
| Fld Name | Fld Cont. |
| MSGFN | 004 |
| KUNNR | 0000100206 |
| RRRNR | nnnnnnn |

*Figure 3.61: IDoc for customer master change*

Good question! And the answer, quite interestingly, is—no. In this case, after change pointers are processed you would get only one IDoc with the most recent data (i.e. after the change) and it would also have code 004 in the field E1KNA1M-MSGFN.

Sadly, this design can cause a problem with some clueless external systems. The only way to work around this is either to ensure that the change pointers are processed frequently enough or ask the external system (politely) to do an additional check on whether the record already exists or needs to be created.

## Not all fields are included

Note that some fields, such as contact address and long text, are not distributed through the same IDoc as other customer master data.

There are separate message types for the address information, e.g. ADRMAS (check SAP Help article "Business Address Services" for more detail), but there doesn't seem to be a standard solution for long texts, unfortunately.

## Sending all records at once

Change pointers are all fine and dandy, but suppose we started running a new interface and there are already tons of master data records that the other system does not have. Do we have to change all of them to trigger the change pointers and IDocs?

Fortunately, a process exists in SAP to spare us of such silly activities. By using transaction **BD12,** we can generate IDocs for the existing customer master records without changing them (Figure 3.62).

To send out the data only for the specific customer numbers, enter the respective numbers in the CUSTOMER field. We can also enter the specific logical system to avoid "blasting" unsuspecting external systems with the data they don't need.

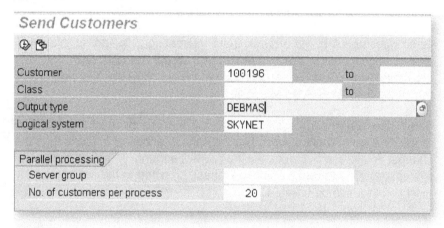

Figure 3.62: Send existing customer records

This transaction can be used either when a new interface has just been implemented (it's a good idea to run it first, before any changes are made in the master data) or when, for any reason, the data between the sender and recipient system gets out of sync.

### Send other master data

Similar transactions exist for other master data, e.g. BD10 is used to send the material master records. To find more similar transaction codes, go to SE93 and search for the codes that start with "BD" (BD*).

## 3.5 Outbound interfaces—conclusion

We have completed the configuration steps for three examples of the most common IDoc interface solutions. As you might have noticed in the interface diagrams, the steps in all the scenarios were very similar (I cleverly used the same drawing with a few changes).

It is important to understand that every IDoc interface will consist of the same or similar building blocks and only the details will change.

▶ If you need to send out transactional data where the condition-based output (transaction NACE) is available, then you can use the output the same way as was described in example 1 (invoice, Section 3.2) and example 2 (purchase order, Section 3.3).

▶ For the interfaces with EDI partners, the output and partner profile configuration described in Section 3.2 applies. For the interfaces with an external system (i.e. logical system) use the partner profile and distribution model configuration described in Section 3.3 and Section 3.4 (examples 2 and 3).

▶ For the master data interfaces where change pointers are available, follow the same steps as in example 3 (Section 3.4). Simply use a different message type, e.g. CREMAS for vendors or MATMAS for material master. The IDoc type is also different, of course, and you use a different transaction to create or change master data.

▶ For the other interfaces briefly mentioned in Section 3.1 but not explained in detail, you will still need to use the common elements described in Chapter 2: port, partner profile, and distribution model (in case of an interface with a logical system). In this chapter, we used output or change pointers to track the created or changed data that needed to be sent out using IDocs. In the interfaces that do not use either of these two techniques, this step is performed by a designated transaction or report.

That's all there is, really!

# 4 Inbound interfaces

In this chapter, we will learn about the inbound IDoc interfaces using two examples: receiving a sales order from an EDI partner and receiving a material master data from an external system. We will also find out how to test the inbound interfaces using Test Tool (WE19) or a file.

Configuration for the inbound interfaces is very similar to the outbound interfaces. We will still need a partner profile, but instead of adding outbound parameters we will add inbound parameters. We will also still need to maintain a distribution model to communicate with the logical systems (see Section 2.5).

## 4.1  Example 1—receive EDI sales orders

Yes, I know, I know! Every IDoc book or document uses this same scenario as an example (ugh!). In my defense—it is not only one of the most popular inbound IDoc scenarios (every business needs customer orders, don't they?), but also a great example of a rather complex business transaction interface.

As was pointed out in Section 3.2, EDI interfaces usually involve a special application (subsystem or translator) that handles the data translation from the customer's EDI format into the SAP IDoc format.

In this scenario (Figure 4.1), the process starts with the customer creating a purchase order in their own system. Next, the customer sends the purchase order to the EDI subsystem. This subsystem translates it from the customer's EDI format into SAP IDoc format. The IDoc is then processed by a special program in SAP and, as a result, a sales order is created.

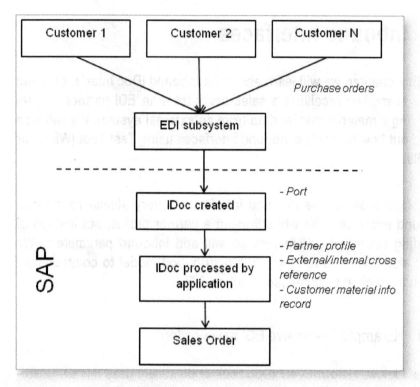

Figure 4.1: Inbound EDI sales order interface example

## EDI order confirmation

 The EDI translator can pass a "functional acknowledgement" back to the customer. But this only confirms the fact that the IDoc was created in SAP successfully. An error might occur in the further IDoc processing and no sales order would be created.

Some companies may choose to provide additional confirmation to the customer after a sales order has been created successfully. To do that in SAP, we can use sales order output and the ORDRSP message type. The configuration for such a confirmation is very similar to the outbound EDI invoice interface example (see Section 3.2).

Specifically with the inbound sales order interface, additional configuration is needed in SAP to handle data conversion. For example, we might need to transform the customer's own material number into the valid SAP material number or convert the partner account number. We will get to it soon, but the first stop, as usual, is the partner profile.

## Partner profile (inbound EDI)

In this scenario, the Sold-to customer is our EDI partner. We have already created a partner profile for a Bill-to party in Section 3.2. You can use the same partner profile and add a new message type to it or create a new profile.

Go to transaction **WE20**. If you need to create new partner profile, click on the CREATE (☐) icon, then enter the customer account number in the PARTNER NO field and KU (for Customer) in the PARTN. TYPE field (refer to Figure 3.7).

To add an inbound message type, click CREATE INBOUND PARAMETER (☐) underneath the INBOUND PARMTRS table (Figure 4.2).

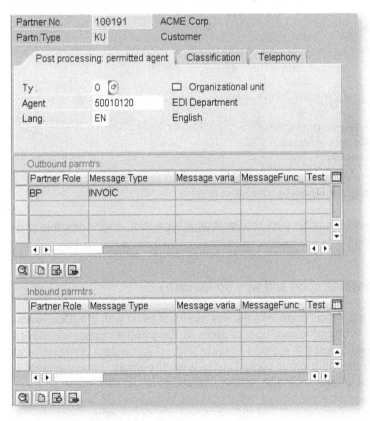

*Figure 4.2: Add inbound parameter to partner profile*

Note that for the inbound message type, we do not specify any port in the partner profile. In the inbound interfaces, the partner profile is used to specify how to process the IDoc **after** it has been created and the port comes into play a bit earlier.

For the inbound messages, there are just two fields to fill in:

▶ MESSAGE TYPE—ORDERS for the sales orders

▶ PROCESS CODE—ORDE

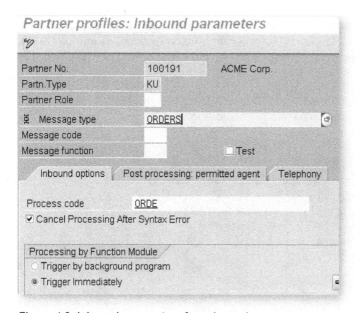

*Figure 4.3: Inbound parameters for sales order*

We are already familiar with the message type, but what does this process code do?

## What is a process code and why do we care?

Simply put, a *process code* tells the system what to do with the IDoc exactly (or, in more official terms, how to process IDoc in the application layer). As I have mentioned a few times already, IDoc is just a data container and does not do anything on its own. That is why it requires the whole entourage of "helpers" like message types or functions to get stuff done.

In the outbound scenarios, we did not need a process code because we were using the output or special transactions to create the IDocs and that is where all the magic happened. In the reverse scenario (i.e. inbound), we receive the IDocs and need to let the system know what to do with them. That's where the process code comes into play.

**Why a process code?**

We already have message type and IDoc type, isn't it enough for SAP to know what to do? Technically, we could manage without it, but process codes offer more flexibility and allow us to perform different activities while using the same message type.

Process codes are maintained in transaction **WE42** (Figure 4.4), but I find that transaction **WE64** (Figure 4.5) is more convenient for browsing because it displays the available process codes by message type.

## Display View "Inbound process code": Overview

| Inbound process code | Description of process |
|---|---|
| ORDE | ORDERS Create sales order |
| ORDE_BY_WORKFLOW | ORDERS sales order with texts |
| ORDM | ORDCHG VMI PO creation confir |
| ORDR | ORDRSP Purchase order confir |

Dialog Structure
- Inbound process code
  - Logical message

*Figure 4.4: Display inbound process codes (WE42)*

## Process codes in IDoc outbound and IDoc inbound

| Messages -> Process cod | Description | Message Type | |
|---|---|---|---|
| ORDERS | Purchase order / order | Direction | Inbox |
| ABI_AIDN_IN | Auto-ID IDOC Process | | |
| ED00 | Display IDoc Using Work Item | | |
| ED00_XML | Display IDoc using work item (XM | Message Type | ORDERS |
| ED08 | Forward IDoc | For all message types | |
| ZABI_DLV_IN | Delivery advice (AIDDESADV with | | |
| DELO | Delivery order (MAIS Pick-up She | | |
| EDX_ORDE | ORDERS Create sales order | Message Variant | |
| ORDE | ORDERS Create sales order | For all message codes | |
| ORDE_BY_WO | ORDERS sales order with texts | | |
| WVFB | ORDERS >= 3.0 or GOODS_RE | | |
| ORDNTF | Internal Communication Between | Message function | |
| ORDRSP | Purchase order / order confirmati | For all message functions | |
| ORDMASTER | Replicate (OreMasterDataReplie | | |

*Figure 4.5: Process codes by message type (WE64)*

Note that we also had to specify a process code in the outbound interfaces with Message Control (Section 3.2 and Section 3.3). For the inbound interfaces, I can only offer the same suggestion on choosing the right process code: pick one from the dropdown list that seems right to you. Also, trust me, you are not the only one confused about this, and so many times the right combination can be easily found online (see Appendix A for search tips).

## Maintain an EDI customer/vendor cross-reference

As we know, to enter a sales order in SAP we need to fill in several required fields, such as order type and sales area (which consists of Sales Organization, Distribution Channel, and Division). Of course, our EDI customer could not care less about such intricacies of the order entry in SAP. It is our problem how to get their order into our system. And we do want to keep our customers happy, so that's why we use transaction **VOE2** to fill in the gap between what the customer sends us and what is required to place an order in SAP.

In this transaction, enter the following (Figure 4.6):

▶ **Customer** – This is the same account number as in the partner profile, i.e. Sold-to partner in this example.

▶ **Vendor** – This is not the SAP vendor master account but the ID in the customer's own system that represents our sales organization as a vendor.

▶ **Sales area fields**: Sales Organization, Distribution Channel, and Division

▶ **Sales order type**

Change View "View for Table EDSDC": Overview

✎ New Entries

| Customer | Vendor number | SOrg. | SOrg description | DChl | DChannel descrip. | Dv | Division descr | SaTy | SD type descrip. |
|---|---|---|---|---|---|---|---|---|---|
| 100191 | | 3000 | USA Philadelphi | 10 | Final customer sales | 00 | Cross-division | OR | Standard Order |
| 301080 | | 3020 | USA Denver | 30 | Internet Sales | 00 | Cross-division | | |
| 301130 | | 3020 | USA Denver | 30 | Internet Sales | 00 | Cross-division | | |
| CP_COMPANY | CPF3 | CPF1 | Sales Org. US | C1 | Direct Sales | 00 | Cross-division | ZCPO | Standard Order |

*Figure 4.6: Transaction VOE2*

The VENDOR NUMBER field in this transaction can be left blank; however, it needs to be filled in when the same customer can place an order for more than one sales area. For example, we can have two sales organizations in the same SAP system. For the EDI customer, these sales organizations are two different vendors.

This information is stored in the database table EDSDC. Note that the primary key in this table is Customer and Vendor, therefore we can only assign one sales area and one sales order type to the same Customer/Vendor combination.

---

### VOE2 and VOE4 in non-modifiable clients

 If you get an error message about client status "not modifiable" when saving an entry in transaction VOE2 then read the SAP KBA **1929600** ("VOE2 and VOE4— Client has status "not modifiable" (TK430)") for the instructions on how to make these tables maintainable in non-modifiable clients. This article applies to VOE2 and VOE4 transactions (VOE4 is discussed in the next section).

---

## Maintain external/internal customer cross-reference

Another important part of the order entry puzzle that our EDI customer expects us to solve is the partner assignment.

At a minimum, Sold-to and Ship-to partners are required to enter a sales order. We already have a Sold-to customer number in the partner profile (this number should be assigned by the EDI subsystem when IDoc is created). But our customer might specify a different Ship-to or another partner type, such as freight forwarder, in their order. Of course, the customer has no idea about the account numbers in our SAP system, so once again it is on us to map the values received in the customer's order (i.e. "external" ones) to the SAP account numbers (i.e. "internal" ones).

To do that, use transaction **VOE4** (SD EDI Conversion). Click NEW ENTRIES to create a new entry and fill in the fields as follows:

- ▶ CUSTOMER—same account number as in the partner profile (usually a Sold-to partner)

► EXT.FUNCTION—partner function (use dropdown). Note that this is simply the partner function code, the field label is a bit misleading.

► EXTERNAL PARTNER—the account number that the customer sends in the EDI order (this could be a DUNS number or customer's own identifier)

► INT.NO—the corresponding SAP account number.

Figure 4.7 shows a Ship-to party cross-reference example. The EDI customer will send us the SHIP_TO as the Ship-to partner identifier and during the IDoc processing it is converted into SAP account number 100191.

Change View "View for Table EDPAR": Overview

New Entries

| Customer | Ext.function | Name | External partner | Int.no. |
|----------|--------------|------|------------------|---------|
| 100191 | SH | Ship-to party | SHIP_TO | 100191 |

Figure 4.7: Transaction VOE4

The partner cross-reference is stored in table EDPAR. In case you get a message about the "non-modifiable" client status when trying to maintain this data, please see the note at the end of the previous section.

## Customer-material info record—VD51

The last but not least piece of the order puzzle is the material number cross reference.

We have our SAP system and the customer has their own system where the same material can be (and most likely is) represented by another identifier. The customer might use GIANT_BALLOON while in our SAP system it is material number 19736783. Or it would be even more interesting if we also had material GIANT_BALLOON in SAP but it meant a completely different balloon. And if we delivered the customer a wrong balloon they probably would not be too pleased. (Customers are usually very particular about their balloon choices.)

To avoid such misunderstanding, we can use the customer-material info record in SAP. To create a new info record, go to transaction **VD51**. On the first screen fill in the fields:

- ► CUSTOMER—same account number as in the partner profile (Sold-to)
- ► SALES ORGANIZATION
- ► DISTRIBUTION CHANNEL

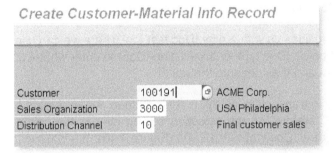

*Figure 4.8: VD51—selection screen*

On the next screen fill in the fields:

- ► MATERIAL NO.—our material number in SAP
- ► CUST. MATERIAL—the corresponding customer's material number

The fields RDPR (Rounding Profile) and UMGR (Unit of Measure Group) are optional.

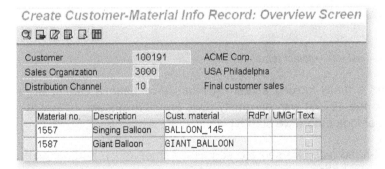

*Figure 4.9: Create customer-material info record*

Save the entry.

To change an existing customer-material info record, use transaction VD52, to display the record, use transaction VD53. This data is stored in the database table KNMT.

## Test an inbound IDoc

In a real-life implementation, we receive an IDoc from the EDI subsystem and do not need to worry about it. But what if we don't have an EDI subsystem and need to run a test?

Fortunately, SAP provides us with a nifty IDoc test tool where we can use a template (based on an IDoc type or an existing IDoc) to enter whatever information we want and then observe the result.

To use this tool, go to transaction **WE19**. In this scenario, we will create a brand new IDoc. Therefore, on the selection screen choose the option BASICTYP and enter the IDoc type ORDERS05 (Figure 4.10).

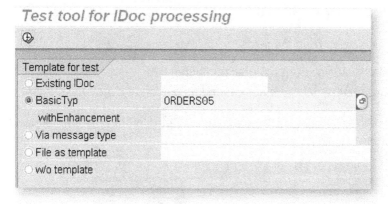

*Figure 4.10: Test tool—select template*

This opens a funny-looking screen (it must have been a cutting edge interface in the 1970s) with an empty IDoc template (Figure 4.11). Let's take a closer look before we start typing in stuff.

On the left-hand side, we see the segment names (such as E1EDK01) and on the right-hand side there is empty space for data entry. The top line labeled EDIDC represents the IDoc control record (it is stored in the EDIDC table). We cannot go anywhere without it, so let's enter something there.

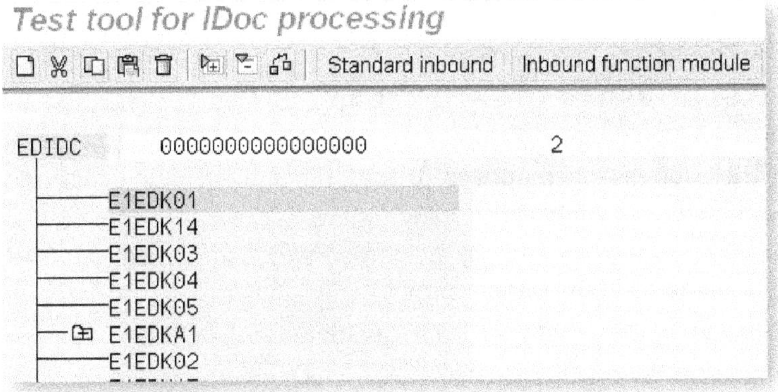

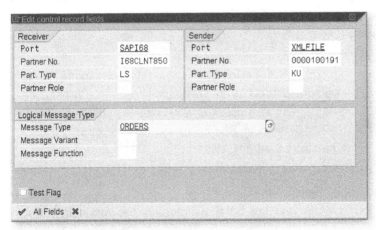

*Figure 4.11: Test tool—blank template*

To fill in the control record, either double-click on the EDIDC label or single click on the light-colored empty space to the right from the label. The pop-up window EDIT CONTROL RECORD FIELDS will appear (Figure 4.12).

*Figure 4.12: Test tool—control record*

In this example, the data receiver is our SAP system and the sender is the EDI customer. Therefore, we need to fill in the control record fields as follows:

> ► RECEIVER PORT—in this case it is not an actual port defined in transaction WE21. Instead, it is a rather peculiar format: the word "SAP" followed by a 3-character system ID. In this example, the system ID is I68, hence the port name is "SAPI68". I don't have any explanation for such naming convention, but it is mentioned casually in the SAP documentation.

- ▶ RECEIVER PARTNER—name of the logical system for the current SAP client (from transaction SCC4)
- ▶ RECEIVER PARTNER TYPE—LS for Logical System
- ▶ SENDER PORT—this can be pretty much any port that exists in WE21, for testing purposes it does not matter. Our usual port XMLFILE works fine in this example.
- ▶ SENDER PARTNER—Sold-to customer account number in SAP (the same as in the partner profile)
- ▶ SENDER PARTNER TYPE—KU for Customer
- ▶ MESSAGE TYPE—ORDERS

Click ✔ to save the entries. Now on to the actual data.

The IDoc segment fields are usually referred to in the same fashion as the database fields in SAP, using dashes. For example, MARA-MATNR means field MATNR in table MARA and E1EDK01-BSART means field BSART in the data segment E1EDK01.

**IDoc segments = data structures**

As a reminder—IDoc data segments correspond to the structure definitions in the Data Dictionary (transaction SE11). For example, if you see an IDoc segment E1EDK01 then in SE11 you will find the structure data type also called E1EDK01.

The data segment content (Figure 4.13) depends on the specific configuration in your system and the bare minimum is the required fields in transaction VA01 (Create sales order). Below are the fields that worked for me, as an example.

At the header level:

- ▶ **Order type** (E1EDK01-BSART). I used standard type OR, but there might be other order type used in your system.
- ▶ **Requested delivery date** (E1EDK03-IDDAT = 002 and E1EDK03-DATUM = date in YYYYMMDD format)

- **Sold-to partner** (E1EDKA1-QUALF = AG, E1EDKA1-KUNNR = customer account number or E1EDKA1-LIFNR = external number if you maintained cross-reference in transaction VOE4)

- **Ship-to partner** (E1EDKA1-QUALF = WE, other fields as for Sold-to partner).

At the item level:

- **Order quantity** (E1EDP01-MENGE)

- **Material number** (E1EDP01-MATNR)

- **Material identifier** (E1EDP19-QUALF = '002', E1EDP19-IDTNR = material number). This segment seems to be redundant, but I was unable to process an order successfully without it. It is also mentioned in several SCN posts, but I could not find a reasonable explanation so far.

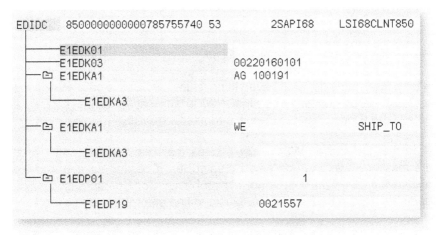

*Figure 4.13: Test tool—data segments*

Naturally, you can also fill in the other data segment fields, as needed. After all the data has been entered, click STANDARD INBOUND in the toolbar to start the IDoc processing.

First, the IDoc control record is checked against the partner profiles. If a matching profile is found, a pop-up window with PARTNER PROFILE FOUND message and a green indicator displays (Figure 4.14).

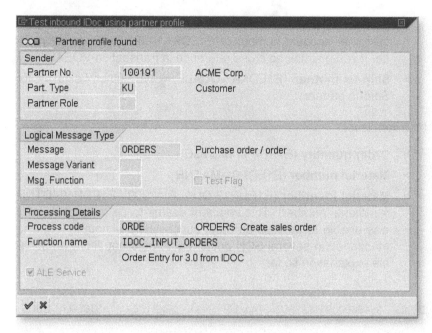

*Figure 4.14: Test tool—partner profile found*

After a few moments, and if everything is fine, an IDoc is created and the message "IDoc number <n> transferred to application" displays. (Take a note of the IDoc number to view it in transaction WE02.)

Note that transaction WE19 only creates the IDoc. That's exactly what the message was saying: "hey, I created the IDoc and passed it to the application layer, the rest is not my problem". Don't be surprised if you open the IDoc in transaction WE02 just to find an error message there.

If the sales order was created successfully, we will see a "green" signal in the IDoc and a status record with status 53 and message V1311 "Standard order ... has been saved" (Figure 4.15).

## The "yellow" status blues?

If you see a "yellow" status instead of a "green" one then simply process the IDoc using transaction BD87, see Section 5.6.

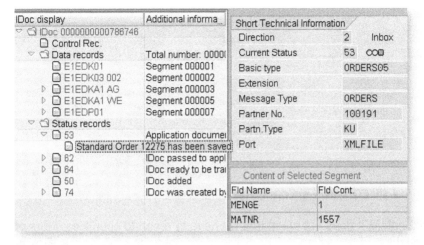

*Figure 4.15: Order IDoc—processed*

But what if there is a problem?

## Trouble in paradise

I will cover IDoc interface troubleshooting and monitoring in more detail in Chapter 5. But that information mostly pertains to the interfaces that have already been implemented in production. From my experience, the challenges while working on the implementation and testing are usually slightly different.

The Test Tool (transaction WE19) validates the partner configuration before creating an IDoc, so at this point errors can only occur in the data conversion or in the depths of the sales order creation functionality.

The most common conversion errors (e.g. sales area, partner or material is invalid or cannot be determined) correspond to the conversion transactions that were mentioned above: VOE2, VOE4, and VD51. If one of these errors occurred, simply add or correct the cross-reference accordingly and then use transaction BD87 to re-process the IDoc.

Other errors are usually the result of incorrect or missing information in the IDoc data segments. But how do you find out what exactly needs to be corrected? To add insult to injury, such error messages can be vague and unhelpful, e. g. "Fill in all required entry fields" (*no, we will not tell you which fields are required, bwahaha!*).

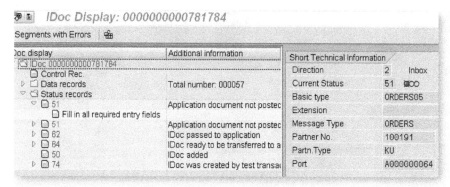

*Figure 4.16: EDI order—error message in the IDoc*

Fortunately, it does not mean that we have to resort to countless hours of debugging. Transaction WE19 provides an option to process the IDoc in the foreground and supplement the missing data.

To use this feature, make a small but significant update in the IDoc control record (labeled EDIDC, as you might recall): check the TEST FLAG checkbox (Figure 4.17).

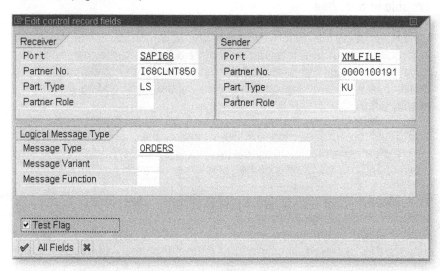

*Figure 4.17: Test tool—control record with Test flag*

Fill in the data segment fields as described above (or as required in your system). To simulate an error, one of the required fields (e.g. Requested Delivery Date, segment E1EDK03) can be left blank.

When the data segments have been filled in, click INBOUND FUNCTION MODULE. This will open the TEST INBOUND IDOC USING A FUNCTION MODULE pop-up. Fill in the fields as follows:

▶ FUNCTION MODULE: IDOC_INPUT_ORDERS (F4 dropdown is available in this field)

▶ In the CALL TRANSACTION PROCESSING area, click the option IN FOREGROUND

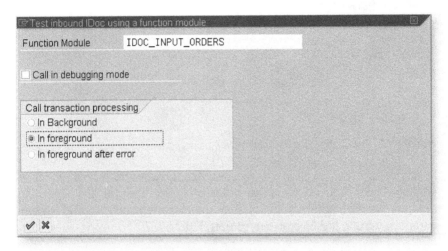

*Figure 4.18: Test IDoc using a function module*

## Looking for a function?

Function module assignment to the IDoc type and message type is maintained in transaction WE57. Function module ABAP code is displayed in transaction SE37.

When we click ✓, the screen that looks suspiciously like transaction VA01 will open (Figure 4.19). We are now inside a *BDC (Batch Data Communication)* recording process. In these recordings, we don't use the regular SAP navigation buttons or menus. Instead, a small pop-up with the field OK-CODE appears and we just need to keep clicking ✓ in that field to move ahead.

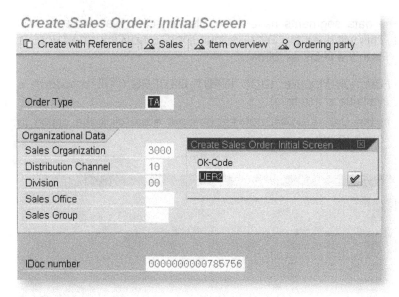

Figure 4.19: Test IDoc—create sales order

In this case I did not fill in the REQUESTED DELIVERY DATE field, which is configured as required for sales order entry. As soon as the recording reaches the problematic field, an error message is displayed and we can manually update the field on the screen (Figure 4.20).

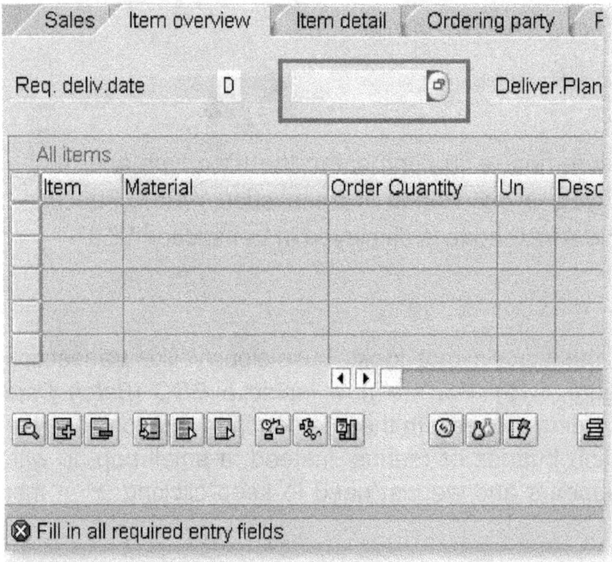

Figure 4.20: Test IDoc—error message

When the end of the recording is reached, the IDoc is created, including the manually updated information. You can use this IDoc as a template for future tests—simply enter an existing IDoc number on the first screen in transaction WE19 (Figure 4.21).

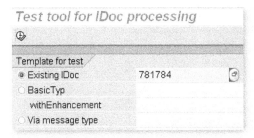

Figure 4.21: Test tool—using existing IDoc as template

---

**Foreground processing is not always available**

Depending on how the IDoc processing function has been written, it might not be feasible to use the foreground processing in transaction WE19, as described. For more details please refer to SAP Help article for transaction WE19 (Test Tool).

---

## Display sales order

When displaying the successfully posted IDoc, we can find the corresponding sales order number in the message under the status record with status 53 (Figure 4.22).

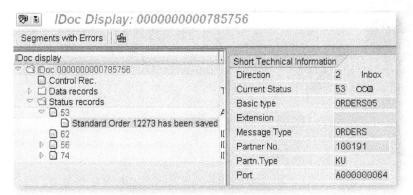

Figure 4.22: Order number in the IDoc status record

107

Sales order can be displayed in transaction **VA03** (Figure 4.23).

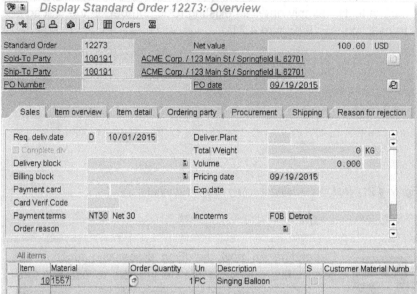

Figure 4.23: Display Sales Order

Note that the familiar SERVICES FOR OBJECT (🦭 🗎) icon is available in both IDoc display (transaction WE02 or WE05) and in transaction VA03. Click this icon and then RELATIONSHIPS to see the corresponding IDoc or sales order entry.

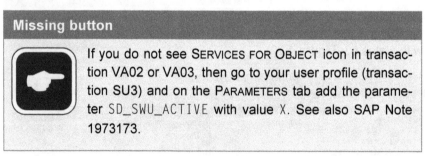

**Missing button**

If you do not see SERVICES FOR OBJECT icon in transaction VA02 or VA03, then go to your user profile (transaction SU3) and on the PARAMETERS tab add the parameter SD_SWU_ACTIVE with value X. See also SAP Note 1973173.

## 4.2 Example 2—receive material master data from an external system

In this scenario, we will pretend to receive the material master data from an external system. This interface will be able to handle the creation of the new material master records and changes in the existing ones.

From the configuration standpoint it is, essentially, the outbound master data example (see Section 3.4) in reverse. And it is even simpler because we don't need to worry about the change pointers. We receive the data, IDoc gets created and processed, and then material data gets created or changed (Figure 4.24).

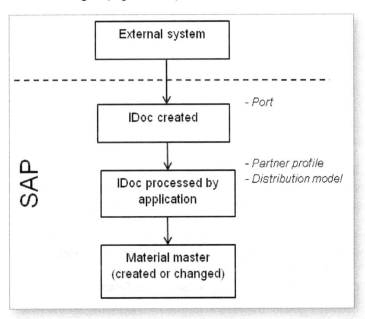

*Figure 4.24: Receive material master data from an external system*

### Change the type—get another master data interface

 You will find that many other inbound master data interfaces are generally the same as this example. The only thing that differs is the message type and IDoc type.

Since this is just an example, and we do not have an actual external system to "talk" to, we need to simulate the data receiving process. For that purpose, we can use the Test Tool (transaction WE19), as in the previous example (Section 4.1). We could start with the message type MATMAS, fill in the required fields, click INBOUND PROCESSING, and repeat the process until we succeed (or patience runs out, whichever comes first).

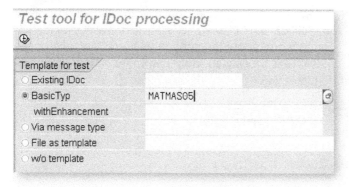

*Figure 4.25: Test tool—create new template*

But for the sake of diversity let's try to use a file instead.

I know this idea does not look very appealing at the first glance. How would we know the file format and isn't it easier to use transaction WE19 and type in some values using a convenient screen interface?

The good news is that we do not actually have to create a file from scratch. We can take a file created by an outbound IDoc, make some changes in it, and "feed" it back to SAP. Even better—you will get to practice the outbound interface skills you learned in Chapter 3!

Here is what we will do:

► configure outbound and inbound interface for material master data (we will update partner profile and distribution model);
► using an existing material, run transaction BD10 to create an IDoc and, consequently, an XML file;
► take that XML file and change some data;
► use the updated file to test the inbound interface and material master creation and change.

Sounds much more fun than plain old Test Tool!

## Partner profile for material master interface

In Chapter 3, we have already created a partner profile for the logical system SKYNET. For this test, we need to add outbound and inbound parameters for the material master data (message type MATMAS) to that partner profile.

Note that in this example outbound parameter is needed only to get a file for testing purposes. This step is not needed in a real-life implementation of an inbound interface.

In transaction **WE20** locate the partner profile for logical system (LS) 'SKYNET' (or create one using instructions in Section 3.3).

To add the outbound parameter (for testing only), click the ⊞ icon underneath the OUTBOUND PARMTRS table (Figure 4.26).

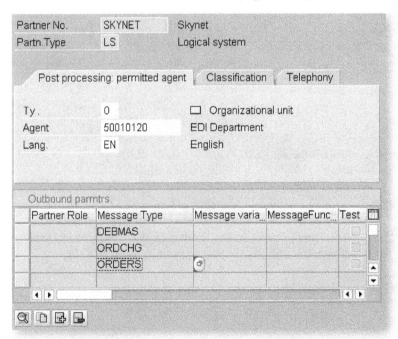

Figure 4.26: Add outbound parameter to partner profile

On the next screen, fill in the fields as follows (Figure 4.27):

- ▶ MESSAGE TYPE—MATMAS
- ▶ RECEIVER PORT—XMLFILE

▶ BASIC TYPE—MATMAS05 (as usual, I chose the IDoc type with the largest number available)

▶ Turn on the TRANSFER IDOC IMMED. option (radio button)

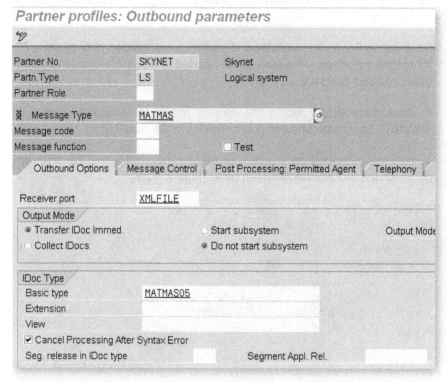

*Figure 4.27: Outbound parameters—MATMAS message type*

Go back to the partner profile screen and click 🗗 underneath the IN-BOUND PARMTRS table to add an inbound parameter (Figure 4.28).

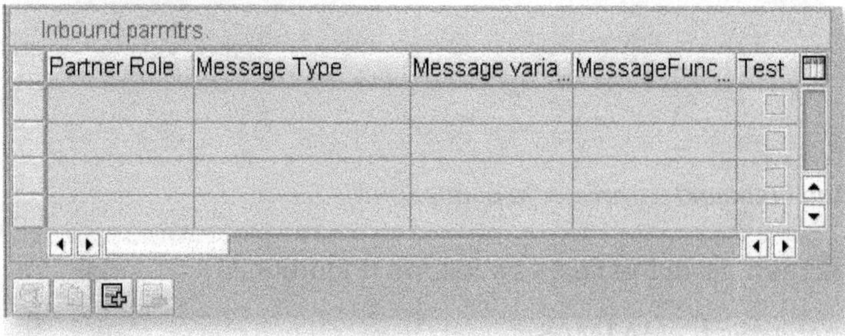

*Figure 4.28: Add inbound parameter to partner profile*

Fill in the fields as follows (Figure 4.29):

▶ MESSAGE TYPE—MATMAS

▶ BASIC TYPE—MATMAS05

▶ Turn on the TRIGGER IMMEDIATELY option

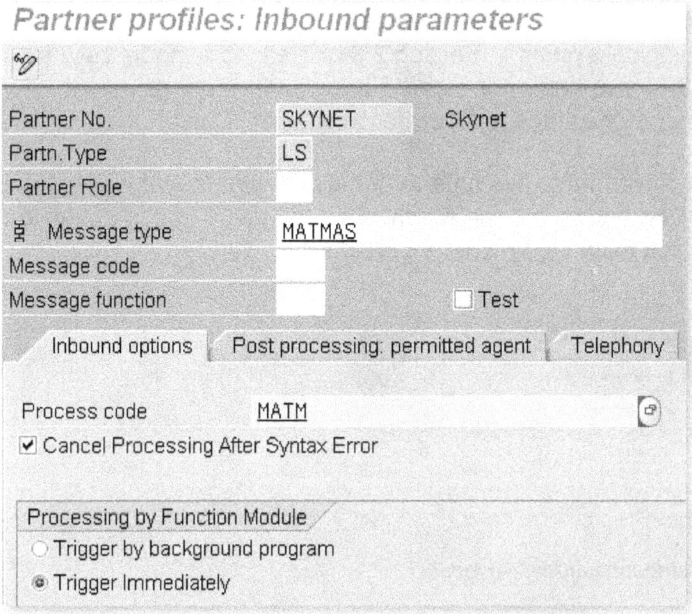

## Partner profiles: Inbound parameters

| Partner No. | SKYNET | Skynet |
| --- | --- | --- |
| Partn.Type | LS | |
| Partner Role | | |
| Message type | MATMAS | |
| Message code | | |
| Message function | | ☐ Test |

| Inbound options | Post processing: permitted agent | Telephony |
| --- | --- | --- |

Process code        MATM

☑ Cancel Processing After Syntax Error

Processing by Function Module
○ Trigger by background program
◉ Trigger Immediately

*Figure 4.29: Inbound parameters—MATMAS message type*

Click 💾 to save the profile.

### Easy view of message type assignment

If there are many message types assigned to a partner profile, it can be difficult to browse them in transaction WE20 (scrolling there is quite painful). Note that this information is stored in database table EDP21 and can be displayed in the Data Viewer (transaction SE16 or SE16N).

## Distribution model for material master interface

As a quick reminder, this example is for an interface with an external system. In SAP, this external system is represented by a logical system (called SKYNET in this book). In addition to the logical system itself, the distribution model is needed for the inbound and outbound interfaces with such systems.

We created a logical system in Section 2.3 and added a model view for it in Section 3.3. If you have not created a logical system or model view yet, please refer to the steps in those sections and create them now.

Now let's add a new message type to the distribution model view. Go to transaction **BD64** and locate the model view (SKYNET in this example). Click 🖉 to switch to change mode (Figure 4.30).

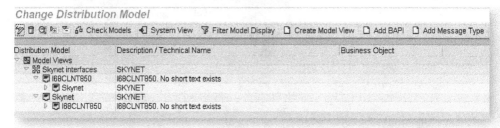

*Figure 4.30: Distribution model—overview*

To get our test file, we will add the outbound configuration (it is almost the same as in Section 3.3 or Section 3.4, only the message type is different). Click ADD MESSAGE TYPE and fill in the fields as follows (Figure 4.31):

- ▶ MODEL VIEW—SKYNET
- ▶ SENDER—logical system assigned to the current SAP client (see transaction SCC4)
- ▶ RECEIVER—our external system, i.e. logical system SKYNET
- ▶ MESSAGE TYPE—MATMAS

114

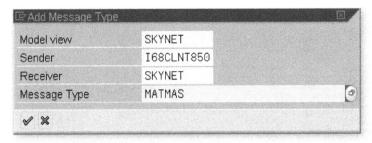

*Figure 4.31: Add outbound message type*

Again, please note that the outbound message type is used here only for testing and it is not needed for a real-life inbound interface.

To add the inbound message, click ADD MESSAGE TYPE and fill in the fields as follows:

▶ MODEL VIEW—SKYNET

▶ SENDER—logical system name for the external system (SKYNET)

▶ RECEIVER—logical system assigned to the current SAP client (see transaction SCC4)

▶ MESSAGE TYPE—MATMAS

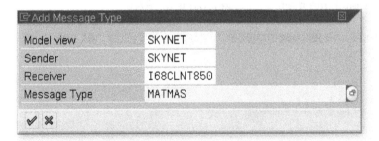

*Figure 4.32: Add inbound message type*

The only difference between the inbound and outbound entries is that RECEIVER and SENDER have switched places.

Overall, the result should look as in Figure 4.33. Save the changes.

115

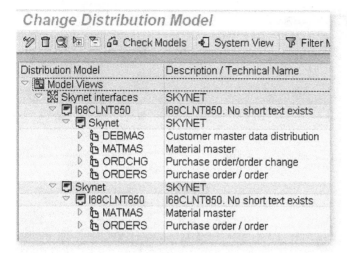

Figure 4.33: Distribution Model—result

## Create the test file

Our configuration is complete; all we need is an existing material master record to use as a guinea pig. Material master records can be viewed in transaction **MM03**; the main database table is MARA.

In this example, we will use material TRANSF-CONT that has only some basic data (Figure 4.34).

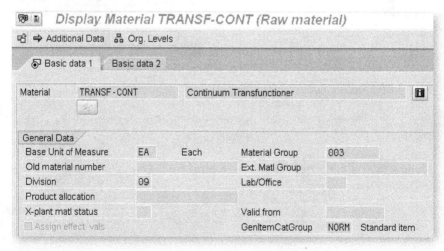

Figure 4.34: Display material (MM03)

We do not need to make any changes in the master data because we will not be using change pointers. In this example, we can use transaction BD10 to create an IDoc for the material without making any changes. How simple is that?

In transaction **BD10**, fill in the fields as follows (Figure 4.35):

▶ MATERIAL—TRANSF-CONT

▶ MESSAGE TYPE—MATMAS

▶ LOGICAL SYSTEM—SKYNET

Click the ⊕ icon to execute the transaction.

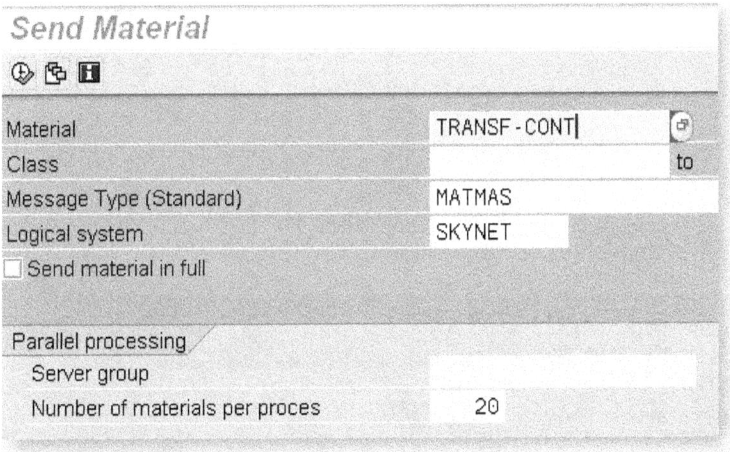

*Figure 4.35: Send material (BD10)*

Because we used the XML file port in the partner profile and chose the "trigger immediately" option, an XML file is created immediately after IDoc creation.

In transaction WE02, we can see the IDoc generated by transaction BD10 (Figure 4.36). The most recent status record (the top one) shows the location of the resulting XML file.

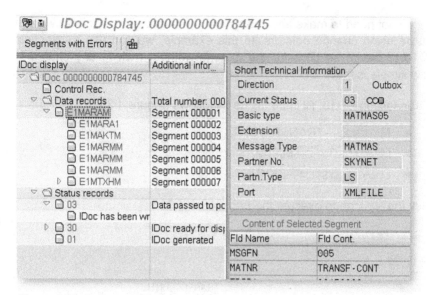

*Figure 4.36: Outbound IDoc generated*

To get the XML file from the SAP application server to a local drive, we can use FTP (if available) or transaction **CG3Y** (Figure 4.37).

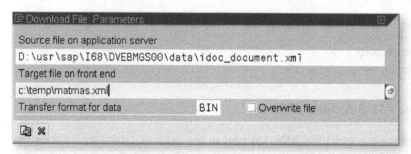

*Figure 4.37: Download file (CG3Y)*

Now that we have the file, we can make some changes in it and then use it to test our inbound interface. If we change the material number in the file then a new material number is created when the file is processed. If we leave the material number as is but change some other fields, then the existing material number is updated.

## Create new material using an XML file

As an experiment, let's change the material number and process the file in SAP. First, I recommend creating a backup copy of the original XML file—we will need it again in the next section. And it is a good practice in general to retain the original just in case.

When working with XML files, I prefer to use XML Notepad editor, but you could use any other suitable application.

Open the XML file and locate node E1MARAM, then field MATNR. Change the material number in this field to a new value, e.g. by adding a suffix '-NEW' at the end. Make sure that no such number exists in the target SAP client.

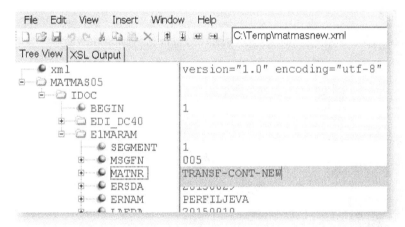

*Figure 4.38: Change XML file to create new material*

**From one client to another**

It is possible to download the file from one SAP client and upload it to another client. In fact, IDocs are quite frequently used to copy master data between SAP clients or SAP systems in the same landscape (e.g. from a QA to a DEV system).

Save the file and upload it back to the SAP application server using either FTP access (if available) or transaction CG3Z (Figure 4.39). Note that the target file location does not have to match any port definition. As usual, when in doubt about the directories available for testing—ask the system administrator.

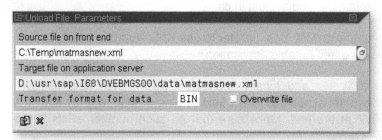

*Figure 4.39: Upload file (CG3Z)*

To process the file, use transaction **WE16**. Fill in the fields as follows:

▶ DIRECTORY + FILE—directory and file name of the test file on the application server

▶ PORT—XMLFILE

*Figure 4.40: Trigger inbound processing (transaction WE16)*

Execute the transaction and, if everything is fine, the message "IDoc file transferred to inbound processing" displays. You can see the new inbound IDoc in transaction WE02 (Figure 4.41).

## Missing: XML file port type

At the moment there is a bug (or a feature?) in transaction WE16.

If you use the search help dropdown ( F4 key) in the PORT field you will only see the file type ports. However, this transaction also works with XML files. To enter an XML type port, type it in instead of using a dropdown.

Also note that the directory and file name do not have to be the same as in the port definition (transaction WE21). The port is needed here only to determine the file format—plain text or XML.

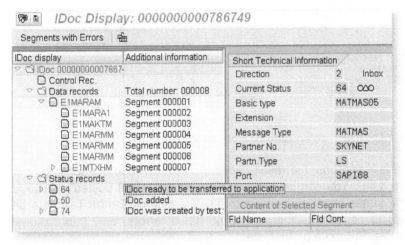

*Figure 4.41: Inbound IDoc for MATMAS message type*

Even though we selected TRANSFER IMMEDIATELY in the partner profile (Figure 4.29), the test IDoc was created with the status 64 ("IDoc ready to be transferred to application"). That is exactly what the message above promised. The yellow signal next to the IDoc status tells us it still needs to be processed.

To process the IDoc, use transaction **BD87** (for additional IDoc processing options see Section 5.10). On the selection screen, enter the IDoc number and leave the other fields blank (Figure 4.42).

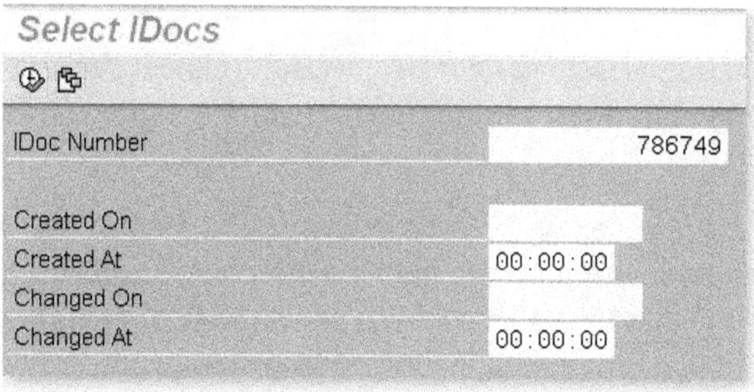

## Select IDocs

⊕ ⓑ

| | |
|---|---|
| IDoc Number | 786749 |

| | |
|---|---|
| Created On | |
| Created At | 00 : 00 : 00 |
| Changed On | |
| Changed At | 00 : 00 : 00 |

*Figure 4.42: BD87—selection screen*

On the next screen, select the line with IDoc status 64 and click the PRO-
CESS button (Figure 4.43).

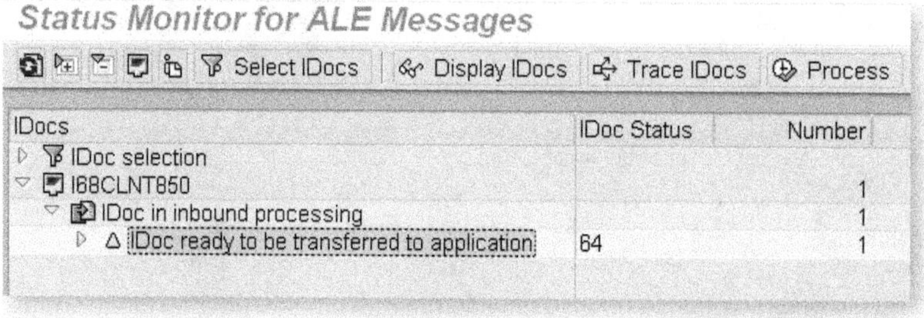

## Status Monitor for ALE Messages

📭 📭 🔁 🖥 🔓 ⅋ Select IDocs | ⅋ Display IDocs ⅋ Trace IDocs ⊕ Process

| IDocs | IDoc Status | Number |
|---|---|---|
| ▷ ⅋ IDoc selection | | |
| ▽ 🖥 I68CLNT850 | | 1 |
| ▽ 📭 IDoc in inbound processing | | 1 |
| ▷ △ IDoc ready to be transferred to application | 64 | 1 |

*Figure 4.43: BD87—select IDoc for processing*

After a few seconds, the results appear on the IDoc PROCESSING screen
(Figure 4.44). You can see the "Application document posted" message
and the status changed from 64 to 53. The column ERROR TEXT is a bit
misleading here since there were no actual errors, only informational
messages. But more on that later.

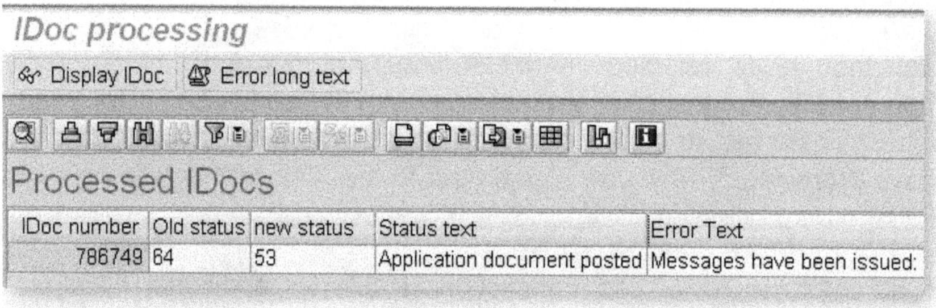

## IDoc processing

⅋ Display IDoc ⅋ Error long text

Ⓠ ⅋ 🖥 🖥 ⅋ ⅋ 🖥🖥🖥 🖥 🖥 🖥

## Processed IDocs

| IDoc number | Old status | new status | Status text | Error Text |
|---|---|---|---|---|
| 786749 | 64 | 53 | Application document posted | Messages have been issued: |

*Figure 4.44: BD87—IDoc processed*

Now that everything has been processed, we can see new material in
transaction MM03 (Figure 4.45).

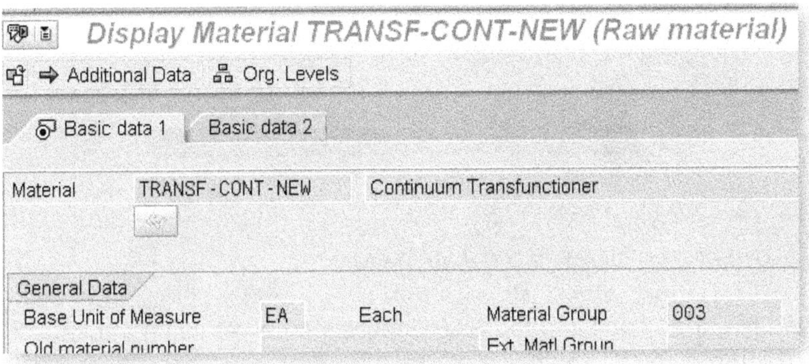

Figure 4.45: MM03—new material created

## Update an existing material using an XML file

For this test, use the original XML file downloaded from the SAP system in the previous section. If you followed the suggestion there, you should have a copy of it. If not—well, tough luck, all is lost now. (Just kidding! Simply run transaction BD10 again and download the file, as we did before.)

Now let's try to make a change in our test material TRANSF-CONT. To do that, we must not change the material number in the XML file (naturally) but change some other field. For example, we can change Gross Weight (field E1MARMM-BRGEW) to 11, see Figure 4.46. Also, since we created new material in the previous test, we might want to change the material description (field E1MAKTM-MAKTX) to note this is an old record, see Figure 4.47.

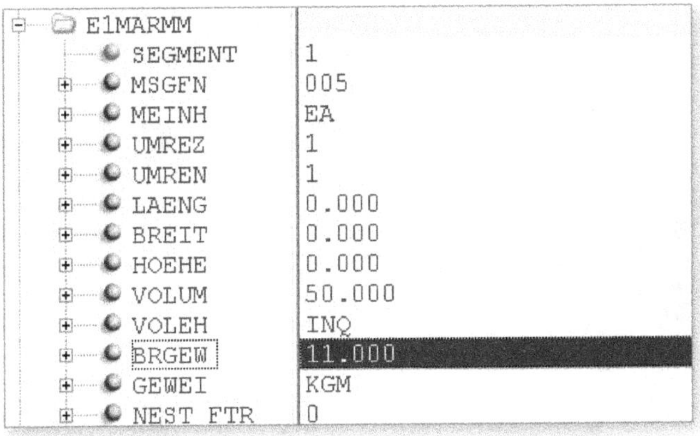

Figure 4.46: XML file, change field E1MARMM-BRGEW

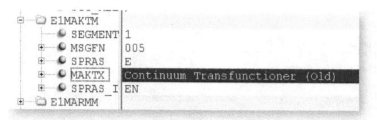

*Figure 4.47: XML file, change field E1MAKTM-MAKTX*

Save the file, then copy it to the SAP application server using transaction CG3Z (Figure 4.39) or another method. After that, run transaction **WE16** again with the new file and the XMLFILE port (see Figure 4.40).

The new IDoc is created (and can be viewed in transaction WE02) with status 64. To process it, repeat the steps in transaction **BD87** as noted in the section above.

The material master has been updated, as we can see in transaction **MM03** (Figure 4.48).

| 🖻 Basic data 1 | 🖻 Basic data 2 | |
|---|---|---|

| Material | TRANSF - CONT | Continuum Transfunctioner (Old) |
|---|---|---|

**General Data**

| | | | | | |
|---|---|---|---|---|---|
| Base Unit of Measure | EA | Each | Material Group | 003 | |
| Old material number | | | Ext. Matl Group | | |
| Division | 09 | | Lab/Office | | |
| Product allocation | | | | | |
| X-plant matl status | | | Valid from | | |
| ☐ Assign effect. vals | | | GenItemCatGroup | NORM | Standar< |

**Material authorization group**

| | |
|---|---|
| Authorization Group | |

**Dimensions/EANs**

| | | | | |
|---|---|---|---|---|
| Gross Weight | 11| | | Weight unit | KG |
| Net Weight | 1 | | | |

*Figure 4.48: MM03—existing material updated*

## View application log

Now let's get back to the "Messages have been issued" warning in transaction BD87. If you double-click on the message, you will find that the IDoc processing log for the material master can be analyzed in transaction **MM90**. We just need the log number from the message (Figure 4.49).

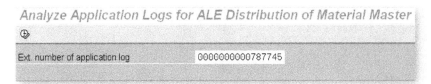

*Figure 4.49: MM90—selection screen*

This log is a list of different messages that occurred during the IDoc processing. Even though there were some warnings (those with "yellow" status), we can see that in the end the material was changed successfully.

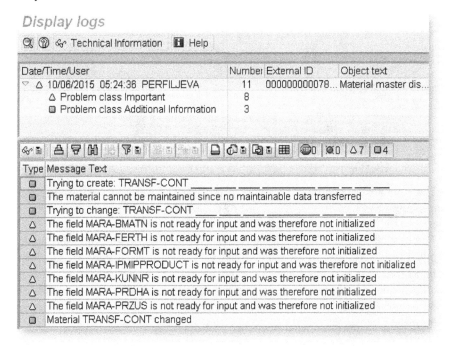

*Figure 4.50: MM90—Display log*

## Test inbound processing with plain text file

Similar testing can be done with a plain text file instead of the XML. This is a rather old-fashioned process, so I will not go into all the details, but the steps are very similar to what we did with the XML file.

Instead of an XML file port, use a file type port (Figure 4.51).

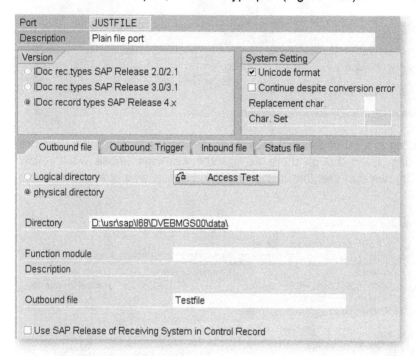

*Figure 4.51: Port for plain text file*

The same port needs to be used in the partner profile for the outbound message type, of course (Figure 4.52).

The text file will look like Figure 4.53. It can be viewed and updated using any text editor that works with plain text files (e.g. Notepad). Keep in mind that this is a fixed-width file, so be very careful not to overwrite or delete any information that can cause incorrect parsing when the file is processed. (That is why XML files are preferable—they are much easier to update, especially using an XML editor.)

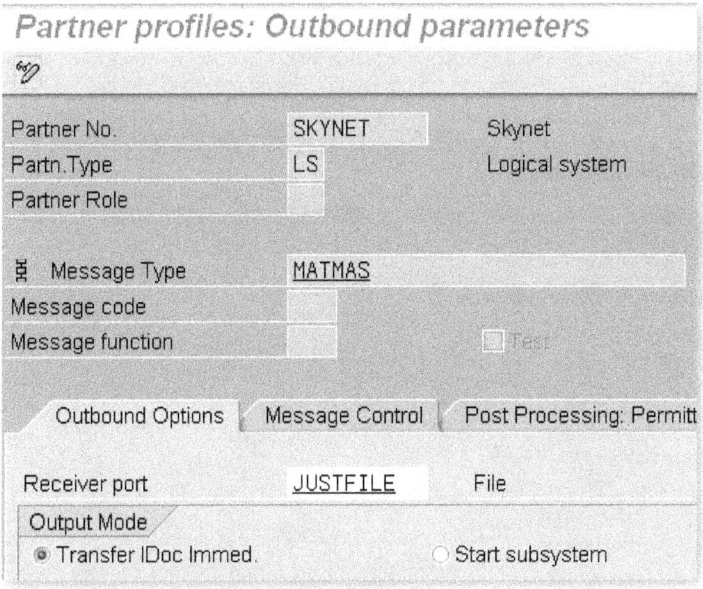

Figure 4.52: Partner profile with plain text port

```
EDI_DC40_U850000000000783745740 3012   MATMAS05
E2MARAM008                             8500000000000783745000001000000002005TRANSF-CONT
E2MARA1005                             8500000000000783745000002000000103
E2MAKTM001                             8500000000000783745000003000000103005EContinuum
E2MARMM004                             8500000000000783745000004000000103005EA 1      1
E2MARMM004                             8500000000000783745000005000000103005KGM1     1
E2MARMM004                             8500000000000783745000006000000103005PCE1     1
E2MTXHM001                             8500000000000783745000007000000103005MATERIAL   T
E2MTXLM                                8500000000000783745000008000000704005* Material
```

Figure 4.53: Plain text file example

To download or upload a file, we can use FTP or transactions CG3Y and CG3Z. Instead of transaction WE16, use transaction **WE12** (Figure 4.54). This transaction has more parameters than WE16 and also requires all the information that we entered in the partner profile above.

The result should be the same—an inbound IDoc and either a new material number created or an existing material number changed, depending on what was changed in the file.

For more information on this functionality, search SAP Help for the article "Test inbound processing—modified outbound file".

127

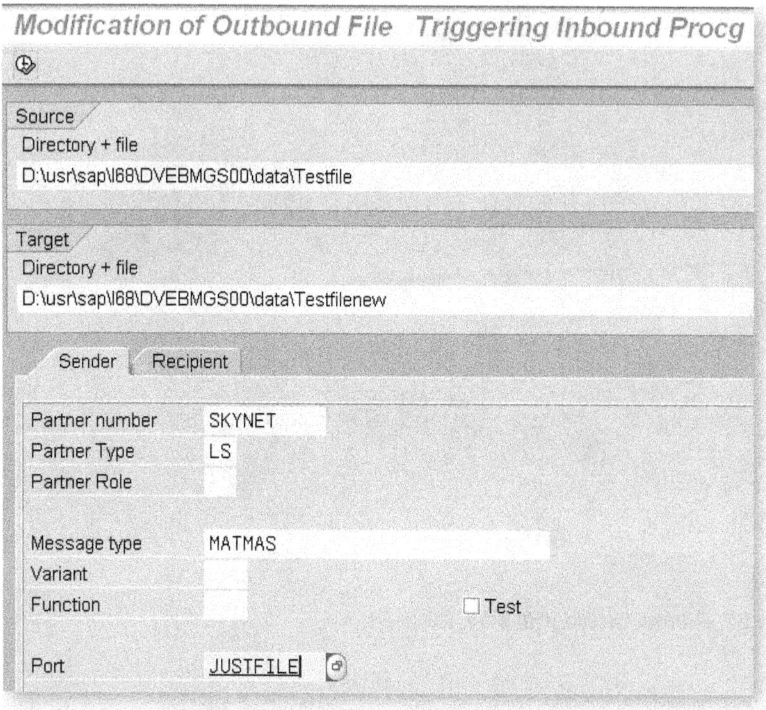

Modification of Outbound File  Triggering Inbound Procg

⊕

Source
Directory + file
D:\usr\sap\I68\DVEBMGS00\data\Testfile

Target
Directory + file
D:\usr\sap\I68\DVEBMGS00\data\Testfilenew

| Sender | Recipient |
| --- | --- |

| Partner number | SKYNET |
| Partner Type | LS |
| Partner Role | |

| Message type | MATMAS |
| Variant | |
| Function | | ☐ Test |

| Port | JUSTFILE ⊡ |

*Figure 4.54: Transaction WE12*

## 4.3  How does an IDoc get into an SAP system?

With outbound interfaces, the process is straightforward: start with some data in SAP, then use the output, change pointers, or another method to create an IDoc. Then the IDoc is processed (by a program, naturally) and —here we go, an XML file. From that point, it is the recipient's problem what they do with that file. (Note: I'm just talking about the examples in this book and don't mean that all outbound IDoc interfaces only create a file. But you get the point.)

With an inbound interface, you are that lucky recipient, so now you have a problem. You have already learned how to configure an interface and process IDocs, but how does an IDoc get into an SAP system in the first place? There are several options.

## Remote function call (RFC)

Personally, I feel that using remote connection is a better option for the inbound IDoc interfaces. When using RFC, an IDoc gets created in SAP immediately, without any additional file processing step in between.

However, this also means that the source system needs to be capable of creating IDocs in SAP using a remote connection. The EDI subsystems and third-party applications designed to interface with SAP usually have this capability.

## File

File interfaces frequently turn into an IT nightmare: files don't get processed, they get accidentally overwritten or lost without a trace, and processed files need to be moved or deleted, and so forth. But in reality, many applications still exist that love sending the files to SAP and will not communicate in any other way.

As shown in Section 4.2 above, we can use both plain text and XML files in the inbound interfaces. But the file format has to match the SAP IDoc type exactly: XML segments have to match the IDoc segments and in the plain text files each line also has to match the IDoc segment structure.

In the example above, we used transactions WE16 and WE12 to process the files. Naturally, in the productive systems this approach will not work since the files need to be processed by a background job without any human intervention. So what do we do?

For the file-based IDoc interfaces, it is best practice to use the "trigger" mechanism. After the file arrives at the desired location (on the SAP application server or other place where it can be accessed in background), a special program *startrfc* can be started to trigger the file processing in SAP.

As an alternative, report RSEINB00 may be run in SAP to process the inbound files periodically, but it works only with the plain text files (port type 3). There seems to be no similar standard program for the XML files.

Many SCN posts suggest using function module IDOC_XML_FROM_ FILE in a custom program to create IDocs from the XML files. However, for the XML format, you might also look into the next option—using HTTP protocol.

But you might ask, "What about the files that do not match the SAP IDoc type format? If a customer sends us a comma-separated file, can we still work with it?" The good news is—yes you can. The bad news—you will need a custom ABAP program to do that.

## XML using the HTTP protocol

As was briefly mentioned in Section 2.1, we also have the XML-HTTP port type available in transaction WE21. The service *idoc_xml* is provided for this purpose and it can be activated or deactivated in transaction **SICF**.

There are two interesting SCN blogs on this subject: "*XML IDoc in SAP ECC Without Middleware and RFC*" by Martin Dejl and "*Post IDoc to SAP ERP over HTTP from any application*" by Grzegorz Glowacki (see Appendix A, page 203). I highly recommend reading them if you are interested in this option.

## Web service

Sadly, there is no simple option in standard SAP to use the web services in the inbound interfaces. Hypothetically, a custom program can be created, but it might make more sense to look into implementing SAP Process Orchestration (formerly known as XI and PI) or another solution.

# 5 Proper care and feeding of the IDoc interfaces

In this chapter, we will learn about monitoring and troubleshooting activities that occur after IDoc interface implementation. We will find how to update and re-process IDocs, analyze output issues, and search for data in the IDocs. The chapter wraps up with a brief overview of IDoc archiving.

## 5.1    IDoc interface ownership: IT or business?

Just like other pesky problems no one wants to deal with, the IDoc interfaces can quickly turn into a tug of war between the IT department and business users. This is especially true when there is a shortage of resources on both sides.

On one hand, business users are not familiar with technical details of the interface configuration, network connections, and such. Also, historically, the interfaces in general have been the realm of IT.

On the other hand, the IDoc interfaces (and the EDI ones in particular) rely heavily on the business data. IT personnel don't usually maintain customer or vendor master data, much less customer material info records. Yet this data (or rather lack thereof) can cause a lot of interface errors.

Unless your organization is fortunate to have designated personnel to monitor and maintain the IDoc interfaces, my suggestion is to work together with the business users on sharing the interface maintenance responsibilities and giving the business users as much of them as possible. (Yes, I work in an IT department, how did you know?)

Business users would be empowered by expanded knowledge and self-sufficiency (also—no more need to talk to the grumpy IT types). And IT personnel would be used more efficiently for complex tasks that actually require their expertise. A win-win, if you ask me.

## 5.2 IDoc interface monitoring options

In the year of 2016 AD, it would be very nice to have a simple option in standard SAP to receive an email upon an IDoc failure. But sorry folks, in the plain vanilla SAP without some wizardry or yet another "solution" no such "easy button" exists. Instead we are stuck with some ho-hum choices.

### Workflow tasks

Remember the "international man of mystery", i.e. the POST-PROCESSING AGENT field in the partner profile? It is possible to configure the workflow tasks to send a work item to the user (or organizational unit) specified in that field. Those lucky people would then go to their SAP Inbox (not to be confused with the email Inbox) and process the work items. Or at least try.

In many cases, a standard task configuration already exists. For example, below is my simple test of a notification for an IDoc failure. (I did not need to do anything other than enter my user ID as "agent" and simulate an error.)

In transaction **SO01** under WORKFLOW node, we can see a notification about an IDoc error (Figure 5.1).

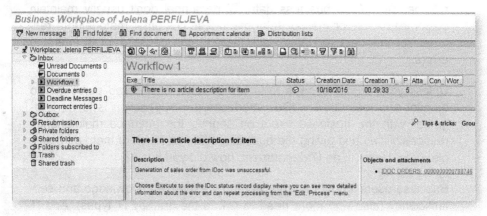

*Figure 5.1: SO01—workflow item*

After double-clicking on the notification, another screen opens with some not-quite-helpful information (Figure 5.2). In this screen, buttons PRO-CESS and DELETE FLAG are available, among others (similar buttons are also available on the previous screen, in the workflow toolbar).

Clicking PROCESS will process the IDoc (this is the equivalent of running transaction BD87, see Section 5.6). Clicking DELETE FLAG will not delete the IDoc, but rather change its status to 68 (Figure 5.3), which means that no further processing is possible even though there was an error.

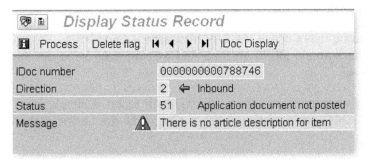

*Figure 5.2: Workflow item detail*

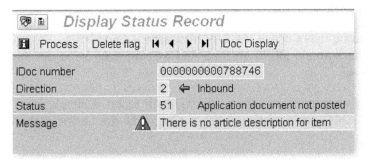

*Figure 5.3: IDoc status change after "Delete flag" action*

The basic setup of workflow notifications for IDocs is explained in the SAP note 116610 (IDoc: Notifications from IDoc processing).

If you are interested in workflow functionality and configuration, please see Appendix A for reference materials.

## Standard SAP transactions

In my experience, people don't usually enjoy going to the SAP Inbox. Many times IDoc interface monitoring simply means periodic execution of transactions such as WE02 or BD87. With these transactions, you can quickly check whether there are any IDocs in status 51 (error) or another status of interest.

## Background jobs

Instead of having users check the SAP transactions periodically, we can schedule a background job to do that. And we can even send out the results by email.

This does not necessarily require a custom ABAP report. A simple query (transaction SQ01) could provide a list of IDocs with the certain status, for example.

For more information on the background jobs see Section 5.11.

## 5.3    Additional features in IDoc display transactions (WE02/WE05)

The IDoc interfaces can be monitored by checking the IDoc List transaction (WE02 or WE05) periodically. This transaction was briefly described in Section 2.7, but there are some additional features that make troubleshooting a bit easier.

On the selection screen in transaction **WE02** or WE05 (Figure 5.4) enter CURRENT STATUS (51 for error) and other selection criteria, as needed. For example:

- ▶ CREATED ON—date range
- ▶ DIRECTION (1 for Outbound or 2 for Inbound)
- ▶ BASIC TYPE—IDoc type, such as ORDERS05
- ▶ LOGICAL MESSAGE—message type, such as ORDERS.

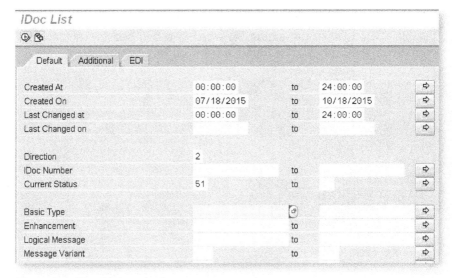

Figure 5.4: IDoc List—selection screen example

## Use wildcard (*) on selection screens

 It's easy to get lost between all the "type" and "message" fields. To avoid any confusion, I use a wildcard (*): ORD* covers both message type (ORDERS) and IDoc type (ORDER05).

This displays a list of IDocs (Figure 5.5), but from the information available here, we cannot tell what the errors are or what to do to resolve them.

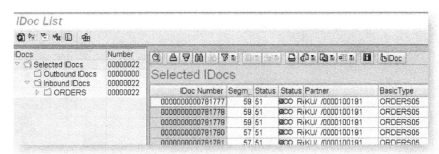

Figure 5.5: IDoc List—IDocs in error

Fortunately, there is a STATUS LIST (✱) icon that switches the display from the plain IDoc list to the status list where we can see the actual error messages (they can also be found in the IDoc status records).

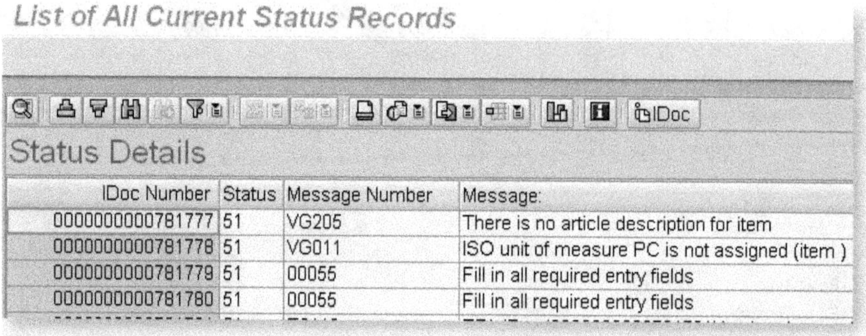

*List of All Current Status Records*

Status Details

| IDoc Number | Status | Message Number | Message: |
|---|---|---|---|
| 0000000000781777 | 51 | VG205 | There is no article description for item |
| 0000000000781778 | 51 | VG011 | ISO unit of measure PC is not assigned (item ) |
| 0000000000781779 | 51 | 00055 | Fill in all required entry fields |
| 0000000000781780 | 51 | 00055 | Fill in all required entry fields |

*Figure 5.6: Status list*

Another useful icon is LIST SPECIFIC SEGMENT (▦). It changes the screen so that the content of the chosen data segment is displayed.

For example, in the EDI invoice scenario (Section 3.2) we can display segment E1EDK01, which includes the invoice number (Figure 5.7). So instead of "something wrong with all these IDocs" list, we get a list of the specific invoice numbers (DOCUMENT column) to look into (Figure 5.8). In my experience, business users generally like invoice numbers more than IDoc numbers.

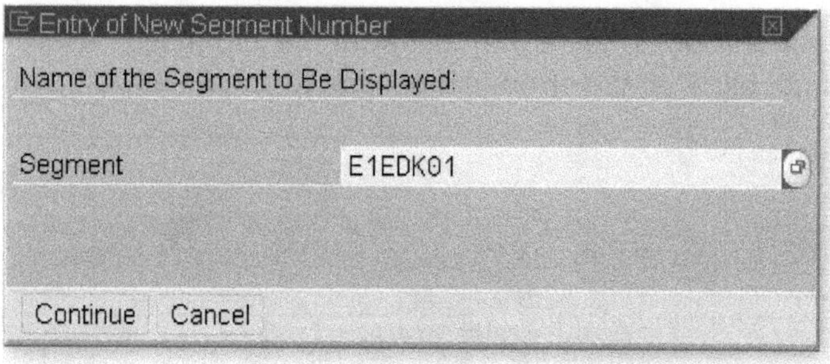

Entry of New Segment Number

Name of the Segment to Be Displayed:

Segment                E1EDK01

Continue    Cancel

*Figure 5.7: Enter segment to be displayed*

Unfortunately, there is no option to re-process the IDocs from this list; for that we have to go to another transaction (see Section 5.6).

*List of All Segments for Segment Names Selected*

| | | | | | | | | | | | | |
|---|---|---|---|---|---|---|---|---|---|---|---|---|
| Q | 🔍 | | 🖨 | ⎙ | 🖩 | — | 🔲 | 📑 | ℹ | 🔲IDoc | | |

SegmentDisplay

| Acti | O | Curr | Curr | Exch.rate | Pmnt terms | Doc.t | Document | Unit | InvLis | Receiver |
|---|---|---|---|---|---|---|---|---|---|---|
| | | USD | USD | 1.00000 | NT30 | INVO | 0090036353 | KGM | LR | 0000100191 |
| | | USD | USD | 1.00000 | NT30 | INVO | 0090036354 | KGM | LR | 0000100191 |
| | | USD | USD | 1.00000 | NT30 | INVO | 0090036353 | KGM | LR | 0000100191 |

*Figure 5.8: Segment Display*

## 5.4   Wanted: IDoc

There are several options to find the IDocs associated with the specific documents.

### Relationship button

As was mentioned in the previous chapters, some transactions have the SERVICES FOR OBJECT icon (🐦 ▪) available. The RELATIONSHIPS node (Figure 5.9) underneath can display the IDocs associated with the document (Figure 5.10). Similarly, in transactions WE02 and WE05 the same icon and node can display the documents associated with the IDoc.

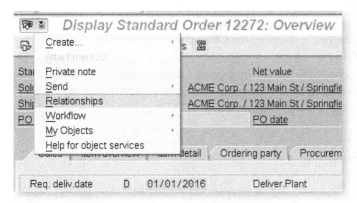

*Figure 5.9: Services for object—Relationships (VA03)*

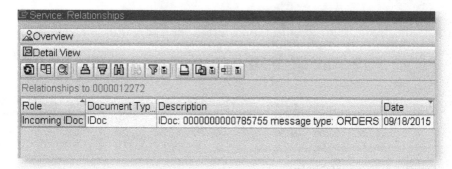

*Figure 5.10: Relationship list in a sales order*

Note that this button is not available in all the transactions and also it may not be visible to users who don't have the authorization or a parameter in the user profile (see SAP note 1973173).

This "magic button" is part of the *Generic Object Services (GOS)* concept. You can find more information on this in SAP Help or online by searching for "GOS" or "object services".

## IDoc List

If the SERVICES FOR OBJECT icon is not available, we might be able to simply search for an IDoc in transaction WE02 or WE05 by date and time.

For example, if a sales order was created by an IDoc, then we can look up the order creation date and time in transaction VA03 and search for the IDocs created or changed just before that. Or when looking for an IDoc associated with a change in a document or master data, check the change documents (usually accessible from the menu) to find the date and time when the change was made.

## Output processing log

If an outbound IDoc was created by an output, check the processing log in the output screen (see Figure 3.16 for example).

## 5.5 Searching for data within IDocs

A customer is calling to find out when their EDI purchase order will be delivered. Customer service cannot find any sales orders for this purchase order. There are two hundred unprocessed IDocs from last night because of a job failure.

What happened to the customer's purchase order? Did we receive an IDoc in SAP or could it be stuck in the EDI translator?

We can use transactions WE02 or WE05 to display specific IDoc segments, but what if we need to find an IDoc quickly?

This is where transaction **WE09** comes in handy. If it does not have the longest selection screen in SAP, then it is definitely in Top 10. How big is this selection screen? It is so big that I could not fit it into one screenshot!

| WE09 and WE10 |
|---|
| 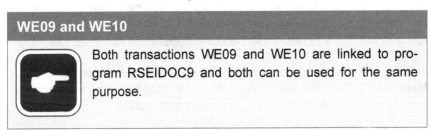 Both transactions WE09 and WE10 are linked to program RSEIDOC9 and both can be used for the same purpose. |

Figure 5.11 and Figure 5.12 show an example of the WE09 selection screen. In this example "MY_ORDER" is the purchase order number and I am searching for inbound IDocs with message type ORDERS.

```
IDoc Search for Business Content

 ⊕ ⅊ 囲 Data Source...

Criteria for Search in Control Records
   Created At              00:00:00        to    24:00:00          ⇨
   Created On              10/01/2015      to    10/18/2015        ⇨
   Last Changed At         00:00:00        to    24:00:00          ⇨
   Last Changed On                         to                      ⇨

   Direction (1=Outb., 2=Inb.)   2         to                      ⇨
   IDoc Number                              to                      ⇨
   Current Status                           to                      ⇨

   Basic Type                               to                      ⇨
   Enhancement                              to                      ⇨
   Logical Message        ORDERS          🔄                        ⇨
```

*Figure 5.11: WE09—selection criteria for control record*

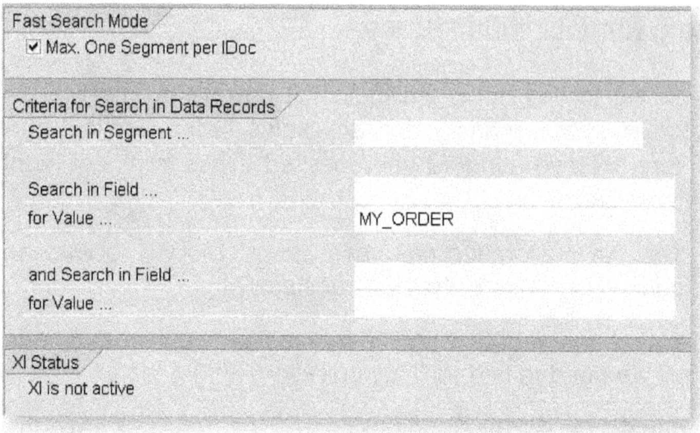

Fast Search Mode
   ☑ Max. One Segment per IDoc

Criteria for Search in Data Records
   Search in Segment ...

   Search in Field ...
   for Value ...                              MY_ORDER

   and Search in Field ..
   for Value ...

XI Status
   XI is not active

*Figure 5.12: WE09—selection criteria for data records*

Note that even though I did not specify the segment name (E1EDK02) the transaction found the IDoc (Figure 5.13). There were not so many IDocs in the IDES system I used and the transaction ran quite fast.

In the productive environment, such a search can be time consuming. Make sure to limit the selection as much as possible using a date range, partner number, segment name, and other parameters.

IDoc Search for Business Content

| IDoc number | Date | Time | Direction | Partner | Status | Descr. |
|---|---|---|---|---|---|---|
| Number Segment type | | | | Number Hier.level | | |
| 0000000000788750 10/18/2015 01:01:29 2 | | | | KU/ /0000100191 53 | | Application document posted |

*Figure 5.13: WE09—search results*

## 5.6    IDoc processing and re-processing (BD87)

Transaction **BD87** can be used to process the IDocs that have not been processed yet or could not be processed due to an error.

Options on the BD87 selection screen (Figure 5.14) are similar to the IDoc List (WE02 or WE05) and include message type, IDoc number, status, and date range.

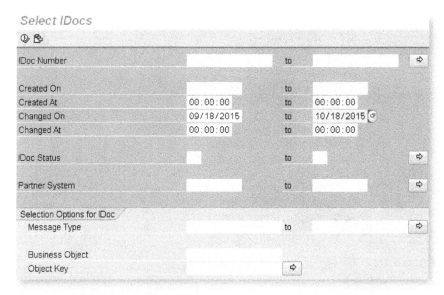

*Figure 5.14: BD87—selection screen*

## Status Monitor for ALE Messages

| IDocs | IDoc Status | Number |
|---|---|---|
| ▽ ▽ IDoc selection | | |
|     ▽ Changed on is in the range 09/18/2015 to 10/18/2015 | | |
| ▽ ▤ I68CLNT850 | | 25 |
|   ▽ IDocs in outbound processing | | 2 |
|     ▷ △ IDoc was edited | 32 | 1 |
|     ▷ ▣ Original of an IDoc which was edited | 33 | 1 |
|   ▽ IDoc in inbound processing | | 23 |
|     ▷ ▨ Application document not posted | 51 | 7 |
|     ▷ ▨ IDoc with errors added | 56 | 2 |
|     ▷ △ IDoc passed to application | 62 | 1 |
|     ▷ ▣ Application document posted | 53 | 9 |
|     ▷ ▣ Error - no further processing | 68 | 3 |
|     ▷ ▣ Original of an IDoc which was edited | 70 | 1 |

*Figure 5.15: BD87—list by status*

On the next screen is an interesting icon 🗊 (called HIGHLIGHT for some reason) that toggles between the display by status (as in Figure 5.15) and display by message type (Figure 5.16).

141

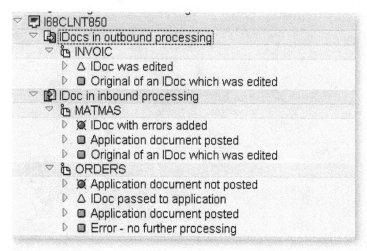

*Figure 5.16: BD87—list by message type*

When using the list by status (Figure 5.15), under the red node APPLICA-TION DOCUMENT NOT POSTED, we can see a hierarchy of message types and error messages.

To see more details under the nodes, simply expand them (Figure 5.17). We can also filter the list by clicking the SELECT IDOCS button.

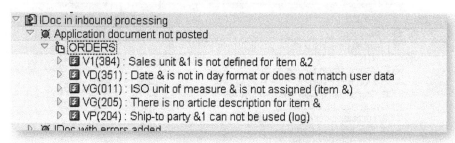

*Figure 5.17: Message type node—expanded*

We can process (or re-process) the IDocs by selecting the hierarchy node that has a "yellow" (not processed) or a "red" (error) status and clicking on PROCESS.

## 5.7    New IDoc Monitor transaction WLF_IDOC

If your SAP system has been upgraded to the certain level of Enhancement Pack (EHP) 5 or 6 then I have great news for you: new transaction **WLF_IDOC** (IDoc Monitor) is available. See SAP note 1724644 for more details but, unfortunately, this transaction cannot be installed using the note and requires the above mentioned EHP and specific support pack (SP) to be applied.

Forget all other transactions—this one is the Holy Grail of the IDoc monitoring. It combines the functionality of WE02/WE05, BD87 and WE09 with additional selections and different presentation options. And—wait for it—it even has the documentation icon (🔲)!

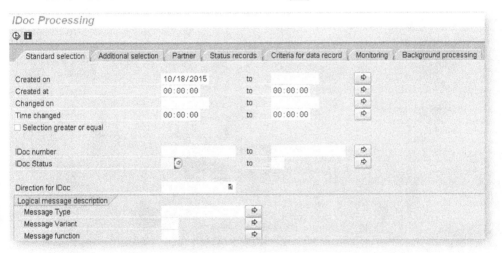

*Figure 5.18: Transaction WLF_IDOC*

## 5.8    Changing IDoc data

Sometimes it may become necessary to change the actual data in the IDoc. For example, a customer could demand specific information (for their own use only) to be included in an EDI invoice. But if we already posted the invoice in SAP then cancelling it could be cumbersome or even not feasible. In such a case, making a change in the IDoc and resending it could save the day.

**Manual changes are not the best practice**

Making changes directly in the IDoc should be an exception rather than regular practice. If manual changes are becoming routine it means something is very wrong with the interface design.

IDocs can be changed in transaction **WE02** (or WE05). Find and open the IDoc in question, then expand the data segments and open the segment that needs to be changed.

Double-click on the CHANGE (▤) icon to the left of the segment name (Figure 5.19). It is important to double-click exactly on that icon and **not** on the segment name.

| IDoc display | Additional inform... | | Short Technical Information | | |
|---|---|---|---|---|---|
| ▤ E1EDK14 008 | Segment 000033 ▲ | | Direction | 1 | Outbox |
| ▤ E1EDK14 015 | Segment 000034 ▼ | | Current Status | 03 | ∞ |
| ▤ E1EDK14 003 | Segment 000035 | | Basic type | INVOIC02 | |
| ▤ E1EDK14 021 | Segment 000036 | | Extension | | |
| ▽ ▤ E1EDP01 | Segment 000037 | | Message Type | INVOIC | |
| ▤ E1EDP02 001 | Segment 000038 | | Partner No. | 100191 | |
| ▤ E1EDP02 002 | Segment 000039 | | Partn.Type | KU | |
| ▤ E1EDP02 016 | Segment 000040 | | Port | XMLFILE | |
| ▤ E1EDP03 029 | Segment 000041 | | | | |
| ▤ E1EDP03 011 | Segment 000042 | | | | |
| ▤ E1EDP03 025 | Segment 000043 | | Content of Selected Segment | | |
| ▤ E1EDP03 027 | Segment 000044 | | | | |
| ▤ E1EDP03 023 | Segment 000045 | | Fld Name | Fld Cont. | |
| ▤ E1EDP03 022 | Segment 000046 | | QUALF | 002 | |
| ▤ E1EDP19 002 | Segment 000047 | | IDTNR | 000000000000001557 | |
| ▤ E1EDP26 003 | Segment 000048 | | KTEXT | Giant Rubber Band | |
| ▤ E1EDP26 010 | Segment 000049 | | | | |
| ▤ E1EDP26 011 | Segment 000050 | | | | |
| ▤ E1EDP26 012 | Segment 000051 | | | | |
| ▤ E1EDP26 001 | Segment 000052 | | | | |

*Figure 5.19: Changing IDoc segment*

A new screen (DISPLAY DATA RECORD FOR IDOC) displays with the segment data presented in table form (Figure 5.20). Go to the menu DATA RECORD • DISPLAY⇨CHANGE. The message "Changes to the IDoc are written to the database" displays. Hit the ⌷Enter⌷ key to close it.

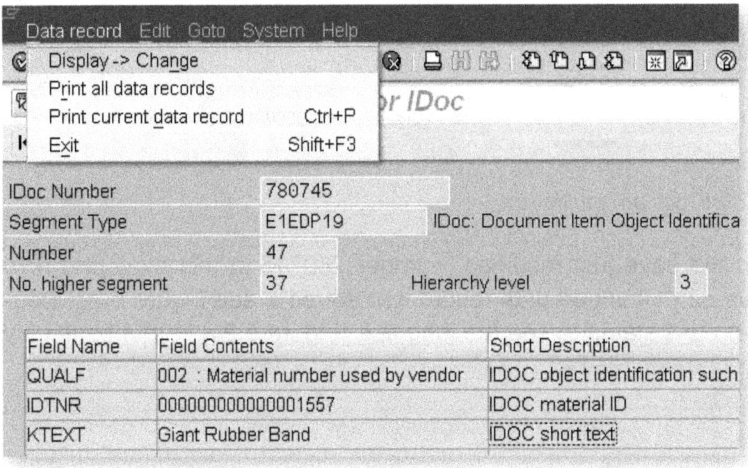

*Figure 5.20: IDoc data record display screen*

The screen title will change to EDIT DATA RECORD. This screen is now in change mode (Figure 5.21). Make the necessary changes in the segment fields and click SAVE when done.

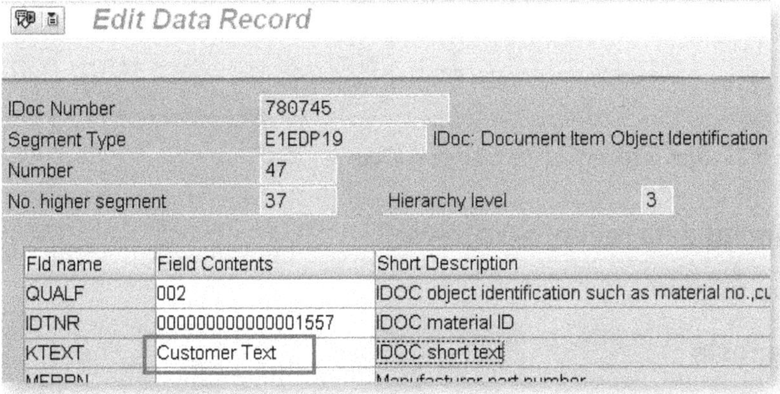

*Figure 5.21: Changing the segment field*

After saving, go back to the IDoc list and click REFRESH. Notice that the list now shows two IDocs with status 32 and 33 (Figure 5.22). What happened here?

## Selected IDocs

| IDoc Number | Segmen | Status | Stat. Gr. | | Partner | BasicType | |
|---|---|---|---|---|---|---|---|
| 0000000000780745 | 60 | 32 | ○△○ | Y | KU/RE/0000100191 | INVOIC02 | |
| 0000000000789745 | 60 | 33 | ○○■ | Green | KU/RE/0000100191 | INVOIC02 | |

*Figure 5.22: IDocs are multiplying!*

The IDoc we have just modified (number 780745 in this example) now has status 32 ("Changed data record was saved"), see Figure 5.23. Double-click on this status to see the long text (Figure 5.24), it mentions new IDoc with number 789745.

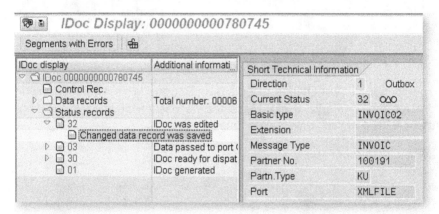

*Figure 5.23: Status record of the changed IDoc*

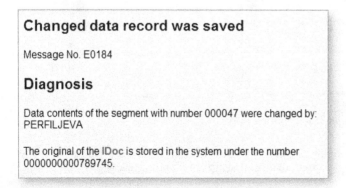

**Changed data record was saved**

Message No. E0184

**Diagnosis**

Data contents of the segment with number 000047 were changed by: PERFILJEVA

The original of the IDoc is stored in the system under the number 0000000000789745.

*Figure 5.24: Status 32—long text*

This newly created IDoc has status 33 (Figure 5.25). As the status description suggests, this is a copy of the original data that was in IDoc 780745 before we changed it. If something went wrong with our changes,

146

we can go back to this copy and check what was in the IDoc before. This also allows tracking of who made a change and when.

**Statuses—Inbound and outbound**

Status 32 and status 33 are used for the edited and original version of the outbound IDocs. For the inbound IDocs, status 69 and status 70 serve the same purpose.

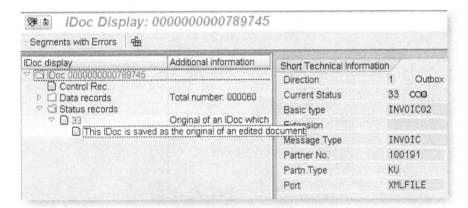

*Figure 5.25: Original data—IDoc status 33*

The IDoc with status 32 can be processed using transaction BD87.

**Not all IDocs can be changed**

Some IDocs cannot be changed using the described technique. For example, we cannot change data in the inbound IDocs that have already been successfully processed (status 53). If an IDoc cannot be changed, then an error message is displayed when accessing the CHANGE menu.

## 5.9    Output troubleshooting

Output management (transaction NACE) is an entirely separate subject, but it is closely related to many outbound IDoc interfaces (see Chapter 3). It is actually not a complex concept, but some time investment might be needed to be able to "connect the dots". Otherwise it can become confusing very quickly. Below, you will find the most common output problems and solutions.

## I am unable to add output manually

The output type needs to be added to the output determination procedure and the procedure needs to be assigned to the document type. One of these steps must be missing or incorrect. Note that this must be corrected; it will not be possible to do any further tests if output is not working.

Output determination procedures can be maintained in transaction **NACE**, button PROCEDURES (Figure 5.26). The output procedure assignment to the documents is performed in different configuration areas in transaction SPRO.

### Conditions for Output Control

| Condition records | Procedures | Output types | Access sequences |
|---|---|---|---|

| Application | Description | |
|---|---|---|
| CF | Error Control | |
| CV | Document Management | |
| E1 | Inbound Delivery | |
| EA | Purchasing RFQ | |
| EF | Purchase Order | |

*Figure 5.26: Transaction NACE, main screen*

## Walk before running

Adding output manually is the simplest troubleshooting test in any "missing output" mystery. Make sure to start all your tests by adding output manually. If it does not work, there is no point doing anything further.

## I can add output manually, but now I want it to be created automatically

To get the automatic output proposal, you need to maintain the output condition records. This can be done in transaction NACE (button CONDITION RECORDS, see Figure 5.26) or in the designated transactions, e.g. VV31 for the billing documents or transaction MN04 for the purchase orders.

## My output is "yellow"

Your output is fine, it just has not been processed yet. In the output screen, click the FURTHER DATA button (Figure 5.27) and check the value in the DISPATCH TIME field. If it does not say "Send immediately" then an additional step (running a report or a transaction) is needed to process the output. For testing purposes, I recommend using the "Send immediately" option (see Figure 3.13).

| Invoice (F2) 90036353 (F2) Display: Output | | | | | | |
| --- | --- | --- | --- | --- | --- | --- |
| Communication method | | Processing log | Further data | | | |
| Invoice (F2) | 0090036353 | | | | | |
| Output | | | | | | |
| Stat | Output | Description | Medium | | Fun | Partner |
| ∞ | RD00 | Invoice | EDI | | BP | 100191 |
| ∞ | RD00 | Invoice | EDI | | BP | 100191 |

*Figure 5.27: Output with "yellow" status*

## My output is "red"

In the output screen, click the PROCESSING LOG button and read the error messages in the log (Figure 5.28). Note that some messages may have long text that can be viewed by clicking ②. After correcting the error(s), click REPEAT PROCESSING in the output screen to repeat the output.

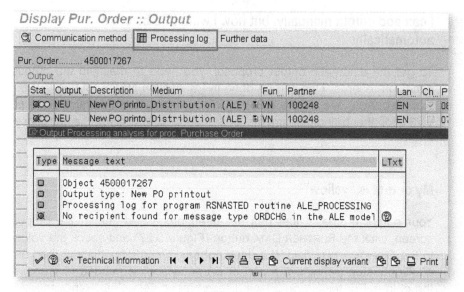

*Figure 5.28: Output with "red" status and processing log*

One of the common mistakes made in the EDI scenarios is mismatching the partner function in the output and in the partner profile. Make sure that a partner profile exists in transaction WE20 for the same partner number and function as in the output.

Also make sure to use "EDI" medium for single partners (customers or vendors) and "ALE" medium for logical systems. And for logical systems, don't forget to maintain the distribution model in addition to the partner profile (see Section 2.3).

## I maintained a condition record but the output is not proposed

Are you able to add output manually? If not, then please see the corresponding question above.

Otherwise, open the document in a change transaction (e. g. VF02 for a billing document), navigate to the MESSAGES screen, and go to the menu GOTO • DETERMIN. ANALYSIS (Figure 5.29).

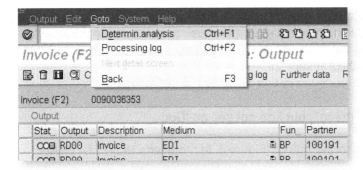

*Figure 5.29: Determination analysis menu*

There you will see how the output condition records are accessed.

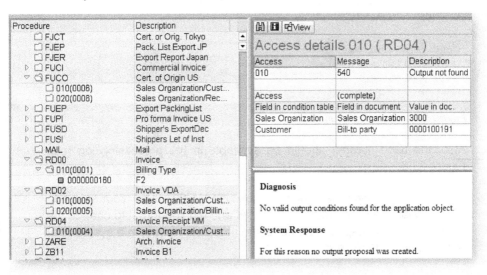

*Figure 5.30: Output determination analysis screen*

Make sure all the access keys are correct and the requirements are passed. For example, billing documents are often assigned requirement 32, which restricts output if the document is not posted to accounting.

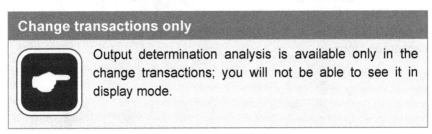

### Change transactions only

Output determination analysis is available only in the change transactions; you will not be able to see it in display mode.

Also, if the output is change related there needs to be actual relevant changes made in the document. In most transactions, you can view changes using the CHANGES menu (it can be located in different places, depending on the transaction).

## My output is "green", but I do not see an IDoc

Check MEDIUM in the output (Figure 5.31); it needs to be EDI or ALE to get an IDoc.

| Invoice (F2) 90036353 | | (F2) Change: Output | | | |
|---|---|---|---|---|---|

📱 🗑 🗈 🔍 Communication method   ⊞ Processing log   Further data   F

Invoice (F2)     0090036353

Output

| Stat | Output | Description | Medium | | Fun | Partner |
|---|---|---|---|---|---|---|
| ∞ | RD00 | Invoice | EDI | 📄 | BP | 100191 |
| ∞ | RD00 | Invoice | Print output | 📄 | BP | 100191 |
| | | | | 📄 | | |

*Figure 5.31: Output medium*

Also, the IDoc number should be available in the processing log (see Figure 3.16).

If you are not finding the IDoc in transaction WE02, check your selection criteria. Was the IDoc created yesterday and did you forget to change the date range? This happens to me all the time when I work in a system that is in a different time zone.

And if the output was created a while ago, the IDoc could already be archived (see Section 5.13).

## 5.10   Background jobs in the IDoc interfaces

In productive systems, the IDoc interfaces are usually handled by the background jobs.

Remember how in the outbound and inbound interface examples in chapters 3 and 4, we always chose the option "trigger immediately" in the partner profile?

This is quite convenient and allows you to speed up the test process. But in a productive system where you might be dealing with a large volume of IDocs and transactions, it can be beneficial to select the other option and then schedule a job to process the IDocs in the background.

In the partner profile (transaction WE20), this option is labeled TRIGGER BY BACKGROUND PROGRAM (Figure 5.32) in the inbound messages and COLLECT IDOCS (Figure 5.33) in the outbound messages.

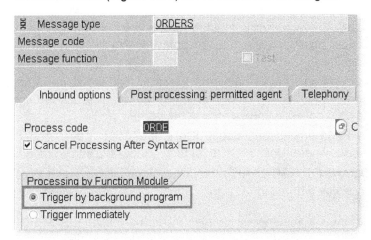

Figure 5.32: Inbound option for background processing

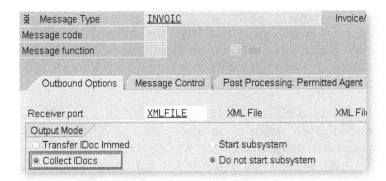

Figure 5.33: Outbound option for background processing

When we use the background processing option, the IDocs are created but not processed immediately. The IDocs are assigned "yellow" status 30 (outbound) or 64 (inbound). The status changes to "green" after the IDocs are processed.

Below are the programs (ABAP reports) that cover the basic processing steps in the inbound and outbound interfaces.

- **RSNAST00** processes output (NAST table). This program is used in the output-based interfaces (like the examples in Section 3.2 and Section 3.3) where output is set to be processed by a background job (output dispatch time is 1 or 2).
- **RBDMIDOC** (same as transaction BD21) processes change pointers. This program is needed for the outbound master data interfaces based on the change pointers, like the example in Section 3.4.
- **RSEOUT00** processes outbound IDocs in "yellow" status. This program is used in the outbound interfaces where IDocs are not set to be processed immediately in the partner profile.
- **RBDAPP01** processes inbound IDocs. It is used in the inbound interfaces where IDocs are not set to be processed immediately.
- **RBDMANIN** or **RBDMANI2** reprocess inbound IDocs that had an error (status 51, "red").

The last program is sometimes scheduled to run right after RBDAPP01 to reprocess any IDocs with errors that were just a side effect of the mass processing.

For example, creation of a goods movement document from an IDoc also locks some of the material master data. If an IDoc containing the same material number is processed at the same exact time (which is not un-common in parallel processing), it will fail because the material master data was locked.

But this is a timing issue that does not require any human intervention to resolve—the IDoc simply needs to be processed again. Report RBD-MANIN can reprocess IDocs at once and eliminate such errors, so that we can concentrate on resolving issues where our intelligence is truly needed.

## 5.11 DIY background job—example

It is very easy to create a background job and there are some cool things we can do with it. However, it is just as easy to create a hot mess if you are not careful (hence the warning).

---

### Exercise caution with background jobs

 When it comes to background jobs, make sure to adhere to company policy, especially in the productive environment. When in doubt—ask for permission and help.

---

In the simple example below, I show you how to create a background job to run standard report RSEOUT00. We will create a selection variant with a dynamic date calculation and then schedule a job to run this report daily and send the result to an email address.

### Create a selection screen variant

Usually the reports have a selection screen and we need to create a variant to use for a background job. But you might find a few programs that do not require this step.

---

### Background jobs—limitations

 It is only possible to schedule the ABAP reports to run in the background. Other objects, such as module pool transactions (e.g. VA01 or MM01) cannot be scheduled to run in a background job.

Also, if the report's functionality requires a GUI to be available (this, unfortunately, includes some ALV reports) it cannot be successfully run in a background job.

---

To create a variant, we need to get to the report's selection screen. The easiest way to do that is with transaction SE38 or SA38—enter the report name (RSEOUT00 in this example) on the first screen and click ⊕. Transaction SE80 can also be used, as well as the designated transactions assigned to the specific reports.

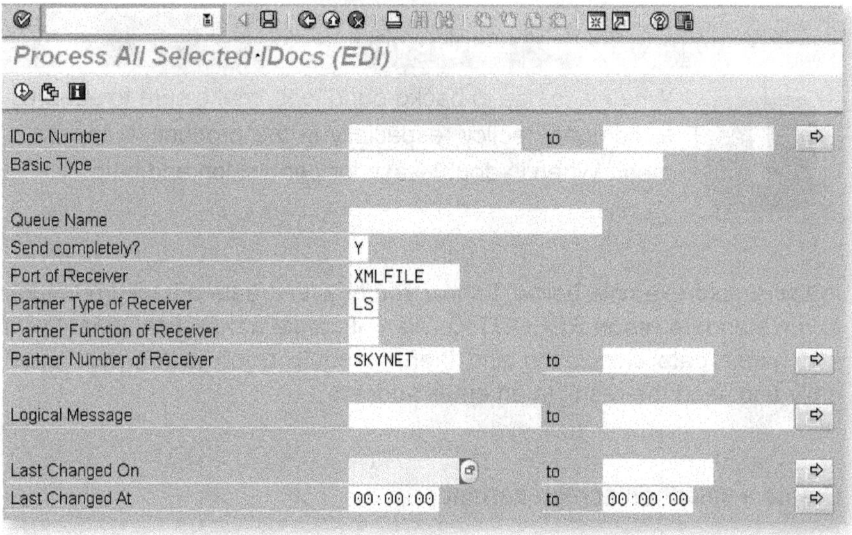

| ⊘ | ⬛ ◁ 🖫 😊 😄 😵 🖵 🖶 🖹 🗐 🗐 🗐 🗐 🖾 🖾 ⑦ 🖶 |
|---|---|

**Process All Selected·IDocs (EDI)**

⊕ 🗐 🗊

| IDoc Number | | to | | ⇨ |
|---|---|---|---|---|
| Basic Type | | | | |
| | | | | |
| Queue Name | | | | |
| Send completely? | Y | | | |
| Port of Receiver | XMLFILE | | | |
| Partner Type of Receiver | LS | | | |
| Partner Function of Receiver | | | | |
| Partner Number of Receiver | SKYNET | to | | ⇨ |
| | | | | |
| Logical Message | | to | | ⇨ |
| | | | | |
| Last Changed On | | ☞ to | | ⇨ |
| Last Changed At | 00:00:00 | to | 00:00:00 | ⇨ |

*Figure 5.34: RSEOUT00—selection screen*

Figure 5.34 shows the selection criteria I chose for the RSEOUT00 report. To create the variant, click the SAVE (🖫) icon on the selection screen.

Then on the VARIANT ATTRIBUTES screen (Figure 5.35), enter the following fields:

▶ VARIANT NAME (BATCH in this example)

▶ DESCRIPTION

On the selection screen we have the field LAST CHANGED ON. If we want the program to look for items that were changed since yesterday, for example, we need to use a dynamic date calculation (today − 1) in the variant. Scroll down the field list until you see the LAST CHANGED ON field and in the same line click on the dropdown in the SELECTION VARIABLE column (see Figure 5.35).

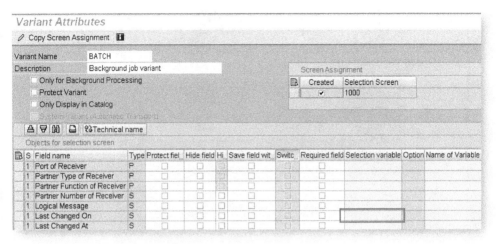

Figure 5.35: Variant attributes

This will open a pop-up window with 3 different choices (Figure 5.36). In this case, we use option X: DYNAMIC DATE CALCULATION (SYSTEM DATE). Option D is the same thing, but it uses local date (based on the user ID). Option T (TABLE VARIABLE) allows all kinds of complex date calculations, such as first and last date of a fiscal period. (Search online for "TVARVC" to find more information on this feature.)

| Type of Variable | Description |
|---|---|
| | Variant Attributes |
| | Choose selection variables |
| T | T: Table Variable from TVARVC |
| D | D: Dynamic Date Calculation (Local Date) |
| X | X: Dynamic Date Calculation (System Date) |

Figure 5.36: Selection variables

Click ✔ to close the window and then click on the dropdown in the NAME OF VARIABLE column (still next to the LAST CHANGED ON field, see Figure 5.35). A new pop-up window will open. This is where it gets a bit tricky.

157

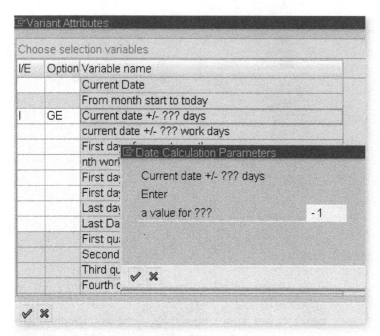

*Figure 5.37: Dynamic date calculation*

In this example, we will use the variable "Current date +/- ??? days" to maintain the date range as "greater or equal to current date - 1 day". To do that, follow this exact sequence of steps:

▶ Click on the dropdown in the I/E column and choose option 'I' (i.e. 'includes')

▶ Click on the dropdown in the OPTION column and choose 'GE' (greater or equals to)

▶ Double-click on the CURRENT DATE +/- ??? DAYS field and in the DATE CALCULATION PARAMETERS pop-up enter - 1.

Click ✓ to close all the pop-ups and get back to the variant screen. The result should look similar to what is shown in Figure 5.38.

| Selection Screen | Field name | Type | Hide field | Selection variable | Option | Name of Variable (Input Only Using F4) | |
|---|---|---|---|---|---|---|---|
| | Objects for selection screen | | | | | | |
| 1,000 | Partner Type of Receiver | P | ☐ | | | | |
| 1,000 | Partner Function of Receiver | P | ☐ | | | | |
| 1,000 | Partner Number of Receiver | S | ☐ | | | | |
| 1,000 | Logical Message | S | ☐ | | | | |
| 1,000 | Last Changed On | S | ☐ | X | ≥ | Current date - 1 days | ⇱ |
| 1,000 | Last Changed At | S | ☐ | | | | |

*Figure 5.38: Selection variable in the variant—result*

## Create background job

Now let's schedule a daily background job with the variant. Go to transaction **SM36** and type in a meaningful job name.

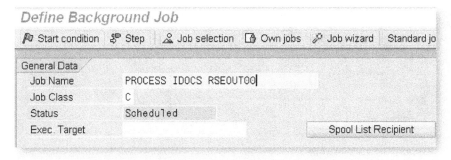

*Figure 5.39: Define background job—main screen*

### My name is Job. Background Job.

In general, I do not recommend including the actual schedule in the job name. A schedule can change and there is nothing more annoying than a job named 'SALES REPORT WEEKLY' that runs every two days.

If there are no special background job naming conventions in your organization, use a name that describes what the job does or identifies the interface.

If the job contains just one step, it is OK to use the program name as the job name, but keep in mind that steps can be changed, too.

Click on the STEP button to add a step to the job and fill in the fields (Figure 5.40):

▶ USER—user ID (there should be a designated user ID for the background jobs, see the warning below)

▶ NAME—report name (RSEOUT00 in this example)

▶ VARIANT—variant name (BATCH, the one we've just created)

Create Step 1

| | |
|---|---|
| User | BATCH |

Program values

| ABAP program | External command |
|---|---|

ABAP program
| | |
|---|---|
| Name | RSEOUT00 |
| Variant | BATCH |
| Language | EN |

*Figure 5.40: Create step*

### Choose the right user for the job

Never use your own or any other dialog user ID in the background job steps, unless it's a one-time run. If the user ID is locked or deleted, it will cause an error when the job runs.

It's not fun at all opening your email in the morning to find 200 failed job alerts because someone thought using their own user ID in a job was a great idea.

Close the window. This will take you to the STEP LIST OVERVIEW screen (Figure 5.41) where you can confirm that the step was added correctly and also add or delete steps should you desire to do so.

Step List Overview

🖉 ☐ 🔍 📇 ⚙ 🗑 🖳 Spool | ⊞ ◄ ◄ ► ►|

| No. | Program name/command | Prog. type | Spool list | Parameters | User | Lang. |
|---|---|---|---|---|---|---|
| 1 | RSEOUT00 | ABAP | | BATCH | BATCH | EN |

*Figure 5.41: Step list overview*

Now go back to the main job screen (Figure 5.39) and click the START CONDITION button.

This will open a pop-up window with the job scheduling options (Figure 5.42). Click the DATE/TIME button and then enter the date and time when the job will run for the first time in SCHEDULED START field. Since we also need this job to run daily, check the PERIODIC JOB checkbox.

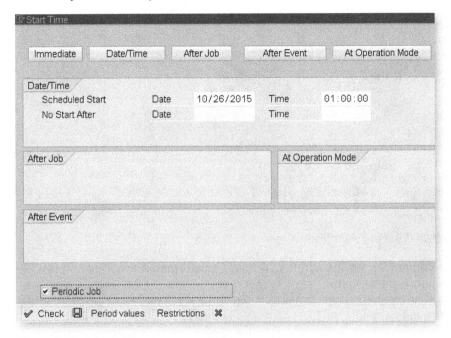

*Figure 5.42: Job start time*

Now click the PERIOD VALUES button and then click the DAILY button (Figure 5.43). You can click the CHECK button to confirm that the schedule is set correctly, then click SAVE twice to get back to the main job screen (Figure 5.39).

*Figure 5.43: Period values*

The result should look like Figure 5.44. Delightful!

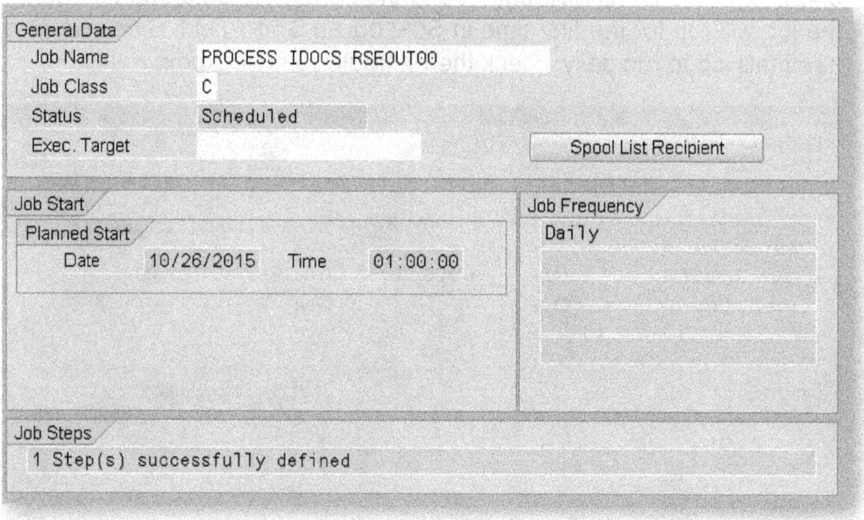

| General Data | |
|---|---|
| Job Name | PROCESS IDOCS RSEOUT00 |
| Job Class | C |
| Status | Scheduled |
| Exec. Target | |

Spool List Recipient

**Job Start**

Planned Start

Date 10/26/2015 Time 01:00:00

**Job Frequency**

Daily

**Job Steps**

1 Step(s) successfully defined

*Figure 5.44: Job overview*

Remember, we also want to send an email when a spool (i.e. report output) is generated as a result of the job run. To set the email recipient(s), click on SPOOL LIST RECIPIENT and then enter the email address in the RECIPIENT field.

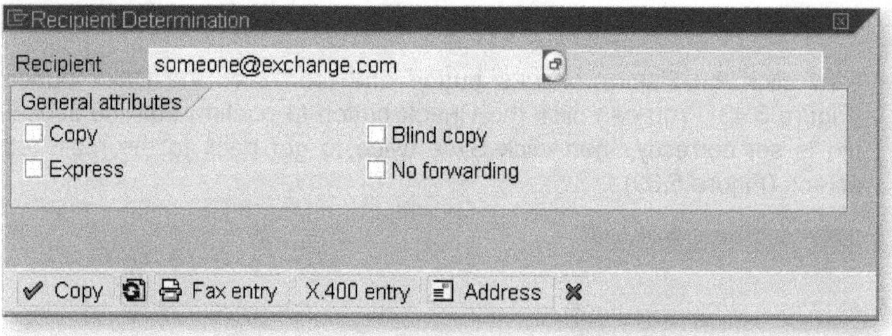

**Recipient Determination**

Recipient    someone@exchange.com

General attributes

☐ Copy                    ☐ Blind copy
☐ Express                 ☐ No forwarding

✓ Copy    🖨 Fax entry    X.400 entry    Address    ✖

*Figure 5.45: Add spool list recipient*

A cool feature here is that as soon as you hit the [Enter] key, the value is recognized as an email address and additional options appear (Figure 5.46).

Make sure to select the ONLY IF NOT RECEIVED radio button to avoid triggering the useless confirmation emails. Click on COPY to close the window.

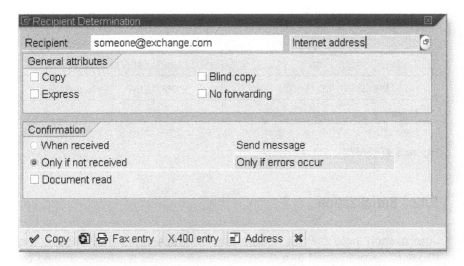

*Figure 5.46: Options for email*

---

**Sending output to multiple recipients**

Spool output can also be sent to multiple emails using a *distribution list*. In SAP systems, distribution lists are maintained in transaction SO24.

Of course, you can also maintain a distribution list externally, on the mail server. Such distribution lists have a single generic email (e.g. GroupOfUsers@company.com), which can be used in the job definition as a regular email address.

---

Now we are back in the main job window. Click SAVE and the job is saved and released immediately. At this point, the job can be viewed in transaction **SM37**. It will remain in "Released" status until the date/time entered in the schedule. Then the job becomes active and later (fingers crossed) completes successfully.

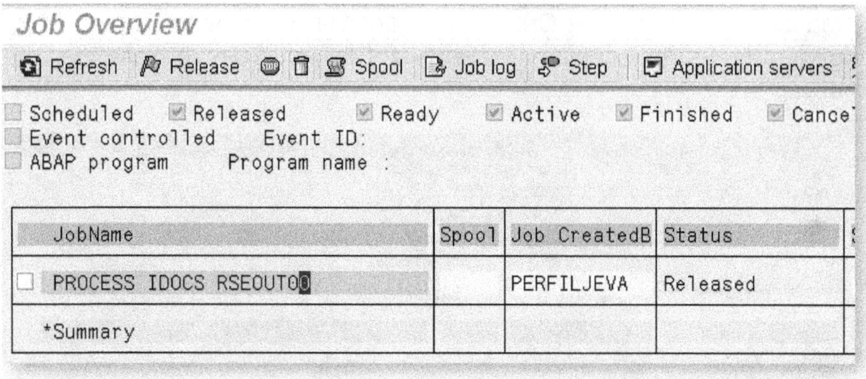

*Figure 5.47: SM37—Job overview*

## 5.12  Serialization

Just a short note on this. Some business scenarios may require the IDocs to be processed in a specific sequence. This is usually caused by dependencies, e.g. we need to have master data before transaction data. Or an order needs to be created before a change in it can be processed.

This concept of building a sequence of IDocs is called *serialization* in SAP. This concept is quite well documented, please refer to the SAP Help article 'Serialization of Messages' for more information.

## 5.13  Archiving

IDoc archiving can easily be a subject of a separate book, but let me briefly introduce the concept.

In general, you will find that archiving in SAP consists of these steps:

- ▶  Data backup (into a file)
- ▶  Actual data deletion from the database

The main archiving transaction in SAP is **SARA**, it is used for transactional and master data as well as IDocs.

Standard reports are also available and can be run in a background job to archive and delete the old IDocs periodically. The reports are:

- **RSEXARCA**—archives the IDocs and writes them into a file
- **RSEXARCB** also writes IDocs into a file similar to RSEXARCA, but is meant to be used for background scheduling. Online documentation is available.
- **RSEXARCD**—deletes the archived IDocs from the database

## IDoc statuses for archiving

 Only the IDocs with archivable statuses can be archived. In transaction WE47 you can display and change archiving settings of each IDoc status.

For this book, I ran a simple test to archive and delete one IDoc. Let me show you the results.

First, I executed the report RSEXARCA with the IDoc number (Figure 5.48). The log was displayed confirming that the IDoc was archived (Figure 5.49).

### IDoc Archiving: Write Program

| IDocs | | |
|---|---|---|
| IDoc number | 782747 | to |

| Restrictions | | |
|---|---|---|
| Created At | 00:00:00 | to |
| Created On | | to |
| Last Changed At | 00:00:00 | to |
| Last Changed on | | to |

*Figure 5.48: IDoc Archiving—selection screen*

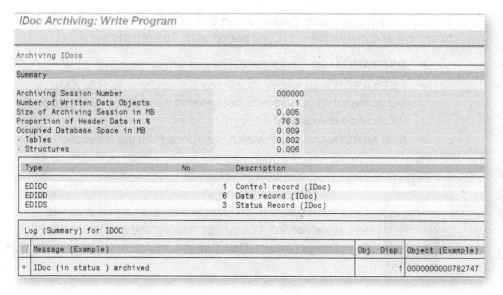

```
IDoc Archiving: Write Program

Archiving IDocs

Summary

Archiving Session Number                      000000
Number of Written Data Objects                     1
Size of Archiving Session in MB               0.005
Proportion of Header Data in %                 76.3
Occupied Database Space in MB                 0.009
- Tables                                      0.002
- Structures                                  0.006
```

| Type | No. | Description |
|------|-----|-------------|
| EDIDC | 1 | Control record (IDoc) |
| EDIDD | 6 | Data record (IDoc) |
| EDIDS | 3 | Status Record (IDoc) |

```
Log (Summary) for IDOC
```

| Message (Example) | Obj. Disp. | Object (Example) |
|-------------------|------------|------------------|
| ♦ IDoc (in status ) archived | 1 | 0000000000782747 |

*Figure 5.49: IDoc Archiving—log*

At this point, I expected the IDoc status to be changed or some other update to happen, but I could not find any differences in the IDoc. Then I tried to run RSEXARCA again, thinking I missed something, but there was no difference.

Reluctantly, I ran the report RSEXARCD with the same IDoc number (Figure 5.50) first in TEST MODE (no updates, only log displayed) and then in PRODUCTION MODE.

```
Deletion Program for Archived IDocs
⊕ 🔁

Processing Options
  ○ Test Mode
  ◉ Production Mode

Detail Log                    No Detail Log              ▤
Log Output                    List                       ▤
```

*Figure 5.50: Archived IDoc deletion—selection screen*

The next screen prompted me for the file selection (remember— archived IDocs are stored in a file). There were two files available because I ran the report RSEXARCA twice (Figure 5.51).

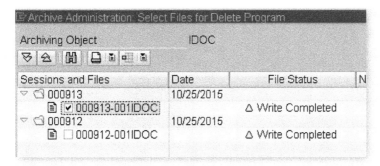

| Archive Administration: Select Files for Delete Program | | | |
|---|---|---|---|
| Archiving Object | IDOC | | |

| Sessions and Files | Date | File Status | N |
|---|---|---|---|
| ▽ 🗂 000913 | 10/25/2015 | | |
| 📄 ☑ 000913-001IDOC | | △ Write Completed | |
| ▽ 🗂 000912 | 10/25/2015 | | |
| 📄 ☐ 000912-001IDOC | | △ Write Completed | |

*Figure 5.51: Archived IDoc deletion—select files*

After that, a log was displayed confirming the IDoc deletion (Figure 5.52). When I checked in transaction WE02, the IDoc no longer existed.

```
Deleted IDocs

Production Mode: Statistics for Deleted Data Objects
Archive File Key                       000913-001IDOC
Number of Deleted Data Objects                    1
Deleted Database Space in MB                   0.004
· Tables                                       0.002
· Cluster                                      0.001
```

| Type | No. | Description |
|---|---|---|
| EDID4 | 6 | IDoc Data Records from 4.0 onwards |
| EDIDC | 1 | Control record (IDoc) |
| EDIDS | 3 | Status Record (IDoc) |

Log (Summary) for IDOC

| Message (Example) | Obj. Disp. | Object (Example) |
|---|---|---|
| ❋ IDoc (with status 03) was deleted | 1 | 0000000000782747 |

*Figure 5.52: IDoc deletion—log*

Additional information on IDoc archiving is available in SAP Help and SAP Notes.

The next screen prompted me for the file (the collection files). Once the IDocs are stored in a file). There were two files available because I ran the report RSEXARCA twice (Figure 5.4).

Figure 5.3 Archived IDoc deletion—select files

Figure 5.4 IDoc relation

Additional information on IDoc archiving is available in SAP Help and SAPNotes.

# 6 When SAP Standard is not enough

In this chapter, we will talk about the IDoc interface enhancement possibilities. We will learn how to extend a standard IDoc by adding a segment to it and how to use inbound and outbound user exits (with invoice and sales order as an example). Also, we will find out how a function module can be used to change the file name dynamically in the IDoc interfaces.

Note that a developer key (obtained from the SAP Support portal) is needed to perform most activities described in this chapter. Also, these changes are transportable—a transport prompt will appear when you save or activate changes.

**Enhance with caution**

Always exercise caution and use good judgement when enhancing an SAP system. All ABAP development should be done by a qualified ABAP developer and follow best practices and development guidelines.

## 6.1 IDoc extension

If the standard IDoc works well, but is missing few fields, we can *extend* it. The IDoc extension process involves the following steps:

- ▶ Create custom segment with additional fields
- ▶ Add custom segment to the extended IDoc type
- ▶ Link extended IDoc type to the standard IDoc and message type
- ▶ Develop a user exit to fill in the new fields (see Section 6.2).

## Outbound and inbound IDoc extension

 IDoc types can be extended for both inbound and outbound processing. However, in the inbound process, we might have limited options for adding the fields because the IDocs are posted by the standard programs that are not aware of our customizations and what to do with them.

This can result in a need to implement multiple user exits or enhancements. In such case, consider carefully whether an IDoc interface is a suitable option for your scenario.

As we know, each IDoc contains data records that consist of data segments. Before going into further details, we need to decide exactly what we are extending and where we want additional fields to appear in the IDoc.

For example, a document might have header- and item-level fields (most documents in SAP are like that: sales order, purchase order, accounting document, you name it). If we want to add some new fields at the header level and some at the item level, then we need two separate custom segments "injected" at two different levels. Also, some data might apply only in certain circumstances and we might need to insert the custom segment as a "child" of the standard segment that it relates to. Simply put—analyze the standard IDoc and decide what it is you need to do before actually doing it. (This sounds like common sense, but you would be surprised how frequently such a simple activity is overlooked.)

In this example, we will create an extension of standard IDoc type INVOIC02 to add a new segment at the line-item level with a BOL (bill of lading) number. This information is stored in the preceding delivery document and therefore is not included in the standard IDoc type. But it is sometimes required by the customers to be included in the invoice IDoc for their reference. Naturally, you can add other fields or extend other IDoc types using the same steps.

---

**IDoc reduction**

You can also remove some fields or whole segments from the standard IDocs. This process is called *IDoc reduction*.

I have not seen any business scenarios so far when this would actually be practical, but it is possible. Refer to SAP Help for more information on the IDoc reduction.

---

## Create a new segment

To create a new custom segment, go to transaction **WE31** (Figure 6.1). In the SEGMENT TYPE field, enter the new segment name (Z1EDP01 in this example) and click CREATE (☐).

---

**Segment naming**

The custom segment name must start with Z or Y, but otherwise there are no special naming conventions. In this example, the custom segment is inserted after standard segment E1EDP01, so I used the same name and just changed the first character.

If there are no other naming conventions in your organization, make sure the segment name is descriptive enough to understand its purpose.

---

*Development segments: Initial screen*

☐ ☐ ⬚ ⬚ ⬚ ⬚ ⬚

| Segment type | Z1EDP01| | | ⬚ |

Definitions

| Version | Segm. definition | Release | Release |
|---------|------------------|---------|---------|
| | | | |

*Figure 6.1: Create new segment type*

171

On the next screen (Figure 6.2), enter the following:

▶ SHORT DESCRIPTION—any informative description
▶ FIELD NAME—BOL_NUMBER
▶ DATA ELEMENT—BOLNR

Save the definition.

*Development segments: Create segment definition*

| | | | | |
|---|---|---|---|---|
| Segment type attributes | | | | |
| Segment type | Z1EDP01 | | ☐ Qualified segment | |
| Short Description | Additional line item fields (E1EDP01) | | | |
| | | | | |
| Segm. definition | | | ☐ Released | |
| | ☐ Primary Segment | | | |
| Last Changed By | | | | |
| Fields in Segment | | | | |

| Posi. | Field Name | Data element | ISO co. | E |
|---|---|---|---|---|
| 1 | BOL_NUMBER | BOLNR | ☐ ☐ | |
| 2 | | | ☐ | |

*Figure 6.2: Add fields to the segment*

Note that only alphanumeric data types (i.e. CHAR, DATS, NUMC, and few others) are allowed in the segments. There are also special considerations regarding number and date formats. For the full list of formatting rules see SAP Help article "Design Guidelines and Formatting Rules for Creating New Segments".

## Segment release

Segments have this rather odd activity called "set release." Every IDoc type (e.g. ORDERS01, ORDERS02) is assigned to the specific SAP Basis or SAP NetWeaver release number. Due to that, custom segments also need to be assigned to the release.

This action is performed in transaction WE31. Enter the segment type and go to the menu EDIT • SET RELEASE (Figure 6.3).

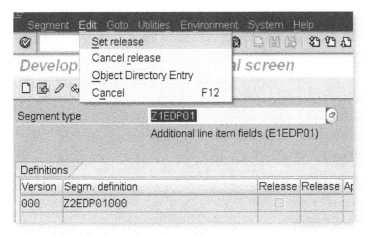

*Figure 6.3: Set release for segment type*

Notice that the RELEASE checkbox becomes checked and the current release number appears in the RELEASE column (Figure 6.4).

After a segment is released, it can no longer be changed. However, until your SAP system has been upgraded to the next release level, you can use menu EDIT • CANCEL RELEASE to cancel the release and continue changing the definition.

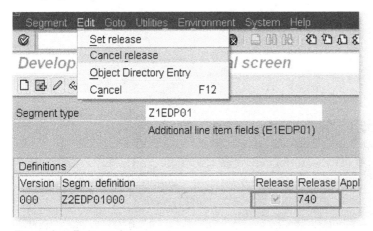

*Figure 6.4: Released segment*

For a while, I thought that as soon as SAP system is upgraded to the next release, the segment definition becomes final. And to some extent that is true—you can no longer change or delete any fields at that time. But it turns out even after an upgrade you can add fields to an existing definition if you click on the ADD VERSION (🔁) icon.

173

This opens the segment definition screen (see Figure 6.2) where you can add more fields. After saving, a new version of the IDoc segment is created with the current SAP release number.

## Create IDoc type extension

In the next step, we need to assign the newly created segment Z1EDP01 to the IDoc type extension.

Go to transaction **WE30** (Figure 6.5) and in the field OBJ. NAME enter the extension name (ZINVOIC02 in this example). In the DEVELOPMENT OBJECT area click the EXTENSION radio button. Then click the CREATE (⬜) icon.

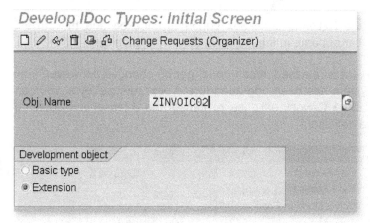

*Figure 6.5: Create IDoc extension*

### Extension naming

IDoc extension names also must start with Z or Y. In this example, we are extending standard IDoc INVOIC02, so for the extension name I just added 'Z'.

Unless there are special internal guidelines, such naming is probably the most practical.

A CREATE EXTENSION window will pop up. Fill in the fields as follows:

▶ Select CREATE NEW option (radio button)

▶ LINKED BASIC TYPE—INVOIC02 in this example

▶ DESCRIPTION—enter any informative description

Click ✔ to continue.

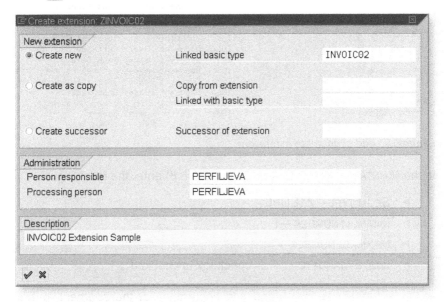

*Figure 6.6: Create new extension from standard IDoc type*

The CREATE EXTENSION screen will appear (it looks very similar to transaction WE19, see Section 4.1). On this screen (Figure 6.7), we need to insert the new segment type in the appropriate place. Since we are adding information at the item level, we add new custom segment as a "child" or E1EDP01 segment.

Place the cursor on the E1EDP01 segment (single click) and click the CREATE (□) icon. The message "Extension segment type(s) will be inserted as child segment type(s) of E1EDP01" displays. This is exactly what we need, hit ⌑Enter⌑ to proceed.

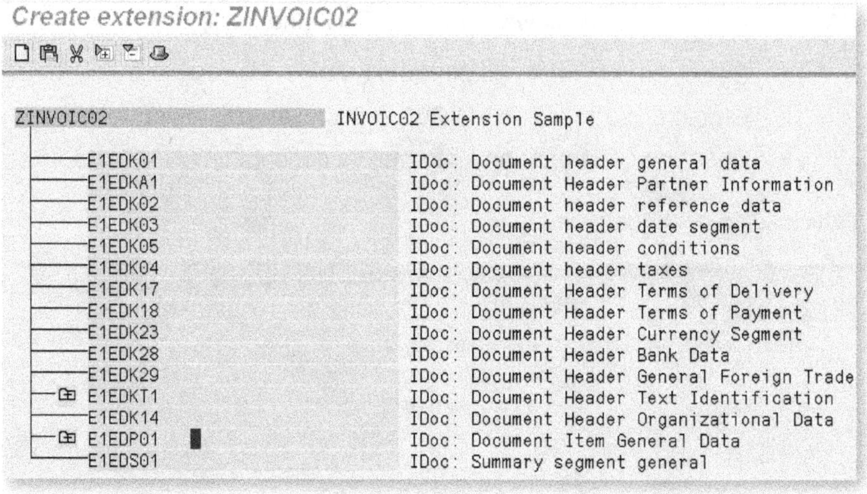

Create extension: ZINVOIC02

ZINVOIC02                              INVOIC02 Extension Sample

```
├──── E1EDK01        IDoc: Document header general data
├──── E1EDKA1        IDoc: Document Header Partner Information
├──── E1EDK02        IDoc: Document header reference data
├──── E1EDK03        IDoc: Document header date segment
├──── E1EDK05        IDoc: Document header conditions
├──── E1EDK04        IDoc: Document header taxes
├──── E1EDK17        IDoc: Document Header Terms of Delivery
├──── E1EDK18        IDoc: Document Header Terms of Payment
├──── E1EDK23        IDoc: Document Header Currency Segment
├──── E1EDK28        IDoc: Document Header Bank Data
├──── E1EDK29        IDoc: Document Header General Foreign Trade
├─ ⊡ E1EDKT1         IDoc: Document Header Text Identification
├──── E1EDK14        IDoc: Document Header Organizational Data
├─ ⊡ E1EDP01  ▌      IDoc: Document Item General Data
└──── E1EDS01        IDoc: Summary segment general
```

*Figure 6.7: Add segment to extension*

In the MAINTAIN ATTRIBUTES window (Figure 6.8) enter the following:

- ▶ SEGM.TYPE—Z1EDP01
- ▶ MINIMUM NUMBER—1
- ▶ MAXIMUM NUMBER—1
- ▶ Leave MANDATORY SEG. checkbox unchecked

In this example, we only need one occurrence of the segment, but in some cases more than one could be needed. For example, in a standard IDoc, the segment with the document texts appears once per text line. In such cases, MAXIMUM NUMBER would be larger, of course. When in doubt, check the documentation for the comparable standard IDoc type and decide from there.

Click ✅ to close the window and save the newly created extension.

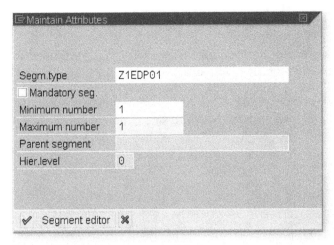

*Figure 6.8: Maintain segment attributes*

## Use the right hierarchy level

If we were adding a new segment at the header level, we would need to add it as a child of a standard header segment (e.g. E1EDK01). In case of a custom partner segment, we would insert it as a child of a standard partner segment (e.g. E1EDKA1), and so forth.

For this reason, we cannot combine the fields of different levels in one custom segment. I.e. if we need to add data at both the header and item levels, we need two separate custom segments created and inserted in two different places.

## Assign an extension to message and IDoc types

Now that we have created the IDoc extension ZINVOIC02, we need to assign it to the standard message type and IDoc type.

This is done in transaction **WE82**. Click on ✎ to switch to the change mode (Figure 6.9) and then click the NEW ENTRIES button to create a new entry.

Change View "Output Types and Assignment to IDoc Types": Overview

✎ New Entries ▯ ▱ ⬿ ▤ ▤ ▯

| Output Types and Assignment to IDoc Types | | | | |
|---|---|---|---|---|
| Message Type | Basic type | Extension | Release | |
| INVOIC | INVOIC01 | | 30A | |
| INVOIC | INVOIC02 | | 40A | |
| INVOIC | INV_ID01 | | 21A | |

*Figure 6.9: Assign extension to message and IDoc type*

On the NEW ENTRIES screen (Figure 6.10) fill in the fields as follows:

▸ MESSAGE TYPE—INVOIC

▸ BASIC TYPE—INVOIC02

▸ EXTENSION—ZINVOIC02

▸ RELEASE—this is the SAP_BASIS component release number starting from which this extension is valid. You can find the current release number using menu SYSTEM • STATUS in any transaction. Use the current release number unless specifically required otherwise.

Save the entry.

New Entries: Overview of Added Entries

✎ ▱ ▤ ▤ ▯

| Output Types and Assignment to IDoc Types | | | |
|---|---|---|---|
| Message Type | Basic type | Extension | Release |
| INVOIC | INVOIC02 | ZINVOIC02 | 740 |
| ☑ | ☑ | | ☑ |
| ☑ | ☑ | | ☑ |

*Figure 6.10: WE82—new entry*

## Assign an extension in a partner profile

To make use of the extension and test an extended IDoc, we need to create or update a partner profile. In this example, we will update the customer (type KU) partner profile that we created in the Section 3.2, but it can be another profile (including LS type), of course.

If we don't add an extension to the partner profile, then for that partner only the "plain" standard IDoc is generated. This feature can actually be convenient because it allows you to limit the use of the extended IDocs and avoid affecting the existing partners.

Go to transaction **WE20** and locate the partner profile. (If you need to create one, follow the instructions in Section 3.2 or Section 3.4) Double-click on the outbound parameter INVOIC to change it.

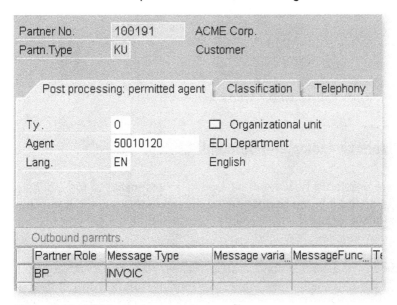

| Partner No. | 100191 | ACME Corp. |
| Partn.Type | KU | Customer |

| Post processing: permitted agent | Classification | Telephony |

| Ty. | 0 | ☐ Organizational unit |
| Agent | 50010120 | EDI Department |
| Lang. | EN | English |

Outbound parmtrs.

| Partner Role | Message Type | Message varia | MessageFunc | Te |
|---|---|---|---|---|
| BP | INVOIC | | | |

*Figure 6.11: WE20—customer partner profile*

Enter ZINVOIC02 (i.e. IDoc extension just created) in the EXTENSION field. Save the profile.

*Partner profiles: Outbound parameters*

| | | | |
|---|---|---|---|
| Partner No. | 100191 | ACME Corp. | |
| Partn.Type | KU | Customer | |
| Partner Role | BP | Bill-to party | |

| Message Type | INVOIC | Invoice/Billing Document |
|---|---|---|
| Message code | | |
| Message function | | ☐ Test |

| Outbound Options | Message Control | Post Processing: Permitted Agent | Telephony | EDI Stan |
|---|---|---|---|---|

| Receiver port | XMLFILE | XML File | XML File |
|---|---|---|---|

**Output Mode**

- ● Transfer IDoc Immed.   ○ Start subsystem            Output Mode    2
- ○ Collect IDocs           ● Do not start subsystem

**IDoc Type**

| Basic type | INVOIC02 | Invoice/Billing document |
|---|---|---|
| Extension | ZINVOIC02 | INVOIC02 Extension Sample |

*Figure 6.12: Outbound parameter—add extension*

## 6.2   User exit example—outbound

So far, we created a new segment, added an extension to the standard type, and added it in the partner profile. Phew! At this point, our configuration is fully functional, but if you try to create a new IDoc you will find that the new segment is empty.

Even though the above configuration makes standard SAP programs aware of the extension, they still do not have a clue how to put data in the custom segment. This means that we need to write some ABAP code and implement a user exit to fill in a new field with some information.

## How to find a user exit for the IDoc

 The easiest way to find a user exit for an IDoc (and I am kidding you not) is to type this question in Google. Actually, if you ask Google "how to find user exit for the IDoc" you will find an answer to that, too.

In a nutshell, to find a user exit, first we need to find the function module for the corresponding message type. Function module names usually include the message type and start with IDOC_INPUT for inbound messages or IDOC_OUTBOUND for outbound messages. For master data interfaces, the function module could also start with MASTERIDOC_CREATE. For instance, we could search for IDOC_OUTBOUND*INVOIC* in transaction SE37.

After locating the function module, find what package it is assigned to (see the ATTRIBUTES tab). Then in transaction SMOD, we can search for the user exits in the same package.

Transaction **SMOD** can be used to view the available enhancements and their components (user exits). Note that these enhancements have nothing to do with the Enhancement Framework in ABAP which was introduced much later.

To implement the IDoc enhancement and user exit, we use transaction **CMOD**. In this transaction, we create a *project*, which is just a placeholder for one or more enhancements.

In this example, we have extended the message type INVOIC. I already found that the right enhancement for the occasion is LVEDF001 and we will need the user exit EXIT_SAPLVEDF_002 in it. (You can easily find the same information using the tip above.)

Go to transaction CMOD, enter the project name (ZEDITEST in this example), and click CREATE (Figure 6.13).

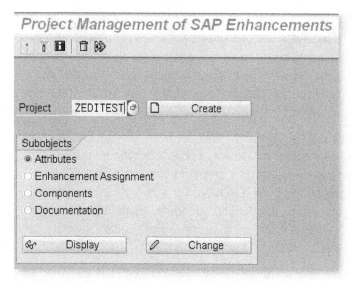

*Figure 6.13: Create enhancement project (CMOD)*

On the next screen, enter the project description in the SHORT TEXT field (Figure 6.14). Save the changes.

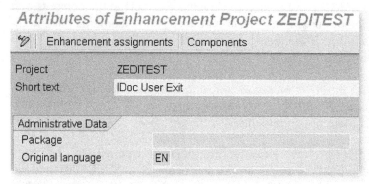

*Figure 6.14: Enhancement project attributes*

Click the ENHANCEMENT ASSIGNMENTS button to open another screen (Figure 6.15). Enter LVEDF001 in the ENHANCEMENT field and save the change.

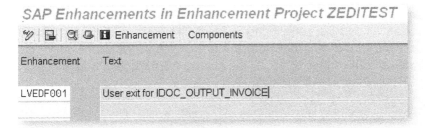

*Figure 6.15: Assign enhancement to project*

Unfortunately, this particular enhancement does not have any documentation, but if it did it could be displayed by clicking ![button].

> ### One enhancement—one project
>
> Enhancements can be assigned only to one project at a time. If you try to assign the same enhancement to another project you will get an error message.

Click the COMPONENTS button. A new screen shows the available user exits (each user exit is a function module). Don't worry about the red signal right now.

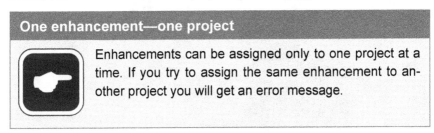

*Figure 6.16: Components (user exits) in the enhancement*

When you double-click on the user exit EXIT_SAPLVEDF_002, the ABAP editor opens and the corresponding function module is displayed. There is no code in the function module except for one INCLUDE line. This include (ZXEDFU02) is where all the custom ABAP code is added.

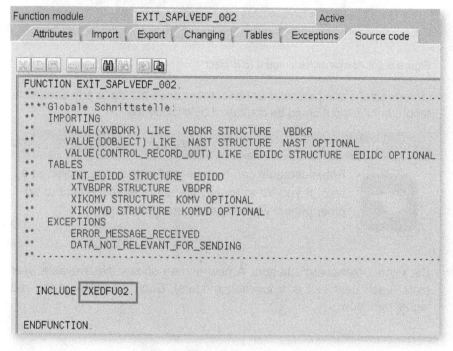

*Figure 6.17: Function module for the user exit*

The next step can be a bit confusing. The include does not actually exist at this point, so you need to create it. To do so, double-click on the include name (ZXEDFU02). The warning message, "Program names ZX... are reserved for includes of exit function groups" will appear at the bottom of the screen. This information is not helpful in any way, so just hit the ⌈Enter⌋ key to move on.

The next message, "Include ZXEDFU02 does not exist. Create Object?" will appear. Click YES. This will give us a brand new blank include named ZXEDFU02 (Figure 6.18).

**Make use of parameters and tables already available**

 I strongly encourage you to check the definitions of all the available parameters and internal tables.

It is very sad to see the developers write ABAP code to read database information that is already available in one of the parameters. Not to mention this is very inefficient and not a good practice in general.

*ABAP Editor: Change Include ZXEDFU02*

| | | |
|---|---|---|
| ← → ⸁ ⸂ ⸃ ⸄ ⸅ · ⸆ ⸇ ⸈ ⸉ ▮ ⸊ ⸋ Pattern Pretty Printer | | |

| Include | ZXEDFU02 | Inactive |
|---|---|---|

```
*.....................................................................*
*    INCLUDE ZXEDFU02                                                 *
*.....................................................................*
|
```

*Figure 6.18: User exit - include*

Here are the parameters and tables available in this user exit.

Parameters (IMPORTING):

▶ XVBDKR—this structure (type VBDKR) contains most of the invoice header data (table VBRK), as well as some header partner data (such as Sold-to and Ship-to name and address).

▶ DOBJECT—this structure (type NAST) includes the output information, such as output type, language, etc. This data is stored in table NAST.

▶ CONTROL_RECORD_OUT—this one represents the IDoc control record (type). It can be used to find the partner ID and type, as well as to identify whether the currently processed IDoc actually includes an extension.

Internal tables available in this include are:

- ▶ INT_EDIDD—this table represents the IDoc data record (structure EDIDD). This is the table needed to modify and populate the custom segment.
- ▶ XTVBDPR—this table (structure VBDPR) represents the invoice item data, i.e. mostly the fields found in the VBRP table. The current line item information is available in the header line of this table.
- ▶ XIKOMV and XIKOMVD (optional) contain pricing information.

This user exit is called as many times as there are standard segments in the IDoc. The current segment name is available in the INT_EDIDD-SEGNAM field (here INT_EDIDD is the header line of the internal table with the same name). The segment data is in the INT_EDIDD-SDATA field. This field is one long string, but for easier access to the individual segment fields, you can move this big chunk of data into the structure that corresponds to the segment name. After making necessary changes, move that structure back into the INT_EDIDD-SDATA field. (This might become clearer after looking at the ABAP code below.)

In this user exit, we can modify data in the standard segments by changing the current record in the INT_EDIDD internal table (it is always the last one). In theory, this should not be needed but, alas, I find that reality is usually different.

We can also add a custom segment by appending a line to the INT_EDIDD internal table. Note that this addition needs to be done when the segment name in the INT_EDIDD-SEGNAM field is the standard segment right **before** the custom one in the IDoc extension. In the example in Section 6.1, we added custom segment ZE1EDP01 right underneath the E1EDP01 segment. Therefore, in the user exit, the code to add ZE1EDP01 should be inside the INT_EDIDD-SEGNAM = 'E1EDP01' condition. I prefer to use the CASE... WHEN... command because every time I try to use IF I end up adding more stuff later and changing it to CASE anyway.

Note that these user exits are triggered for **all** IDocs, not just the extended ones. To make sure the code is executed only for the extended IDocs, we can use the field CONTROL_RECORD_OUT-CIMTYP, for example.

The simple ABAP code below demonstrates how to update the standard segment E1EDP01 (I picked field GRKOR as an example) and add custom segment ZE1EDP01. It is, of course, meant for demonstration purposes only and not necessarily should be copy-pasted by everyone. Always make sure to follow the development guidelines adopted by your organization and general best practices.

**No guidelines? No problem!**

If your organization does not have any ABAP development guidelines, I recommend using the DSAG (German SAP user group) guidelines that are available on the DSAG website.

```
* Execute only for ZINVOIC02
IF control_record_out-cimtyp NE 'ZINVOIC02'.
  RETURN.
ENDIF.

DATA eledp01_data    TYPE eledp01.  " standard segment
DATA zledp01_data    TYPE zledp01.  " custom segment
DATA number_of_lines TYPE i.

CASE int_edidd-segnam.

  WHEN 'E1EDP01'.
* Move segment data into the corresponding structure
    MOVE int_edidd-sdata TO eledp01_data.
    eledp01_data-grkor = '1'.

* Modify segment: move modified data back, find the line
* number and modify it.
    MOVE eledp01_data TO int_edidd-sdata.
    number_of_lines = lines( int_edidd ).
    IF number_of_lines IS NOT INITIAL.
      MODIFY int_edidd INDEX number_of_lines.
    ENDIF.

* Add child segment Z1EDP01: fill in segment name
* and data; add line to the table.
    IF xtvbdpr-vbeln_vl IS NOT INITIAL.  " delivery
      CLEAR: int_edidd.
```

```
      int_edidd-segnam = 'Z1EDP01'.

      SELECT SINGLE bolnr
      INTO z1edp01_data-bol_number
      FROM likp
      WHERE vbeln = xtvbdpr-vbeln_vl.

      MOVE z1edp01_data TO int_edidd-sdata.
      APPEND int_edidd.
    ENDIF.
ENDCASE.
```

*Listing 6.1: ABAP code example for outbound user exit*

After this code has been added to the ZXEDFU02 include, activate the include and navigate back to the CMOD component screen (Figure 6.19). Click ⁀ to activate the user exit and enhancement. If we don't do that, our ABAP code will not work even if the include itself has been activated.

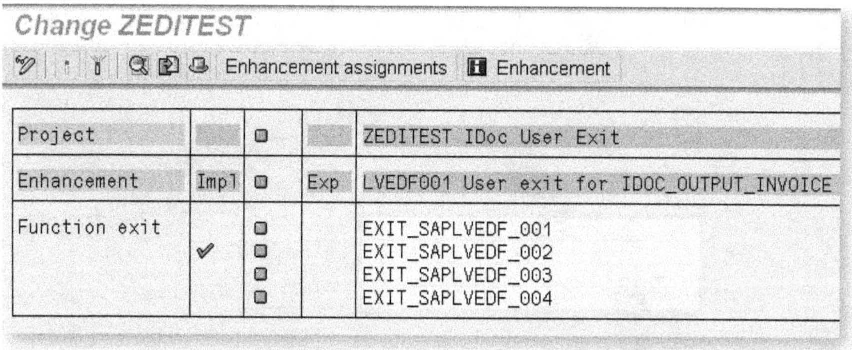

| Change *ZEDITEST* | | | | |
|---|---|---|---|---|
| ✏ ⁀ ⁀ ⊞ 🄳 ⊕ Enhancement assignments 🄷 Enhancement | | | | |
| Project | | ▢ | | ZEDITEST IDoc User Exit |
| Enhancement | Impl | ▢ | Exp | LVEDF001 User exit for IDOC_OUTPUT_INVOICE |
| Function exit | | ▢ | | EXIT_SAPLVEDF_001 |
| | ✔ | ▢ | | EXIT_SAPLVEDF_002 |
| | | ▢ | | EXIT_SAPLVEDF_003 |
| | | ▢ | | EXIT_SAPLVEDF_004 |

*Figure 6.19: Enhancement activated*

---

### Deactivate an enhancement

If for any reason (e.g. troubleshooting) you need to disable the enhancement, you can deactivate it using the corresponding button in transaction CMOD. This will not delete or deactivate the ABAP code; it will only make the user exit unexecutable.

Now everything is ready, so go ahead and create a new IDoc from the invoice output (see Section 3.2 for the steps).

The result should be as shown in Figure 6.20 with the custom segment Z1EDP01 added and the standard segment E1EDP01 updated.

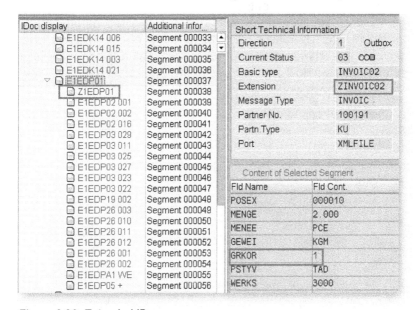

*Figure 6.20: Extended IDoc*

## Debugging—outbound

To debug the user exit, set the breakpoint in the code, for example as shown in Figure 6.21.

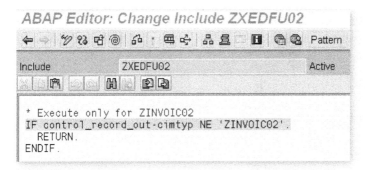

*Figure 6.21 : Debugger breakpoint*

189

In this case, an IDoc is created from the output, but since the output runs in a separate process from the rest of the transaction, it can be rather difficult to use the invoice transaction (VF02) for IDoc user exit debugging. I find the two options below work best.

1. Create an IDoc from the output, as usual (make sure that extension type shows in the IDoc, if not—correct the configuration). In transaction WE19 create a new IDoc as a copy of the existing one. Then click the STANDARD OUTBOUND button to start IDoc processing. The debugger window should open at the breakpoint set in the user exit. This approach works for most IDocs.

2. For the output-based IDocs, use the output processing program RSNAST00. On the selection screen, fill in the fields as in Figure 6.22 (here OBJECT KEY is the invoice number with leading zeroes). Click the ⊕ icon and the debugger window should open at the breakpoint.

| Selection Program for Issuing Output | | | | |
| --- | --- | --- | --- | --- |
| ⊕ ⓑ ⓘ | | | | |
| Selection Param. | | | | |
| Output application | V3 | to | | ⇨ |
| Object key | 0090036353 | to | | ⇨ |
| Output type | RD00 | to | | ⇨ |
| Transmission medium | 6 | to | | ⇨ |
| ☐ Send again | | | | |
| Sort | | | | |

Figure 6.22: RSNAST00 parameters for output debugging

## 6.3   User exit—inbound

As noted in Section 6.1, IDocs can be extended for both outbound and inbound processing. Unfortunately, for the inbound IDocs the process to push the data from the custom segments into SAP is not as straightforward as for outbound IDocs. Specific implementation steps vary greatly depending on the IDoc type. It would be too much material to cover in this short book, but if you are ever in a situation that requires adding new fields to the inbound IDoc, I encourage you to search SAP documentation and the SCN website for information specific to the IDoc type.

In this example, we will see how a user exit can be used in the inbound sales order processing to change the data sent by the customer.

For example, if there were major changes in the material numbers (e. g. due to the legacy system migration or organization realignment), it might take a while before the customers update their records and start sending us valid new material numbers. In the meantime, we can avoid an avalanche of interface errors by converting the material number in an inbound IDoc user exit.

To implement a user exit, go to transaction **CMOD** (Figure 6.23). For the testing purposes, we can use the project ZEDITEST from the outbound example (see Section 6.2) and add an enhancement to it. If you need to create a new project, click the CREATE button, otherwise click the CHANGE button.

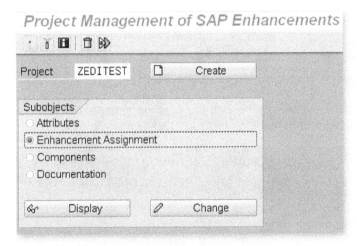

*Figure 6.23: CMOD—project ZEDITEST*

Using the suggestion in Section 6.2, we can identify that the enhancement name for the ORDERS message type is VEDA0001. Click the radio button ENHANCEMENT ASSIGNMENTS to add enhancement VEDA0001 to the project. Save the changes.

| SAP Enhancements in Enhancement Project ZEDITEST |
| --- |

| Enhancement | Text |
| --- | --- |
| LVEDF001 | User exit for IDOC_OUTPUT_INVOICE |
| VEDA0001 | SD EDI Incoming Orders (Customer Extensions) |

*Figure 6.24: Add enhancement VEDA0001*

To determine which user exit to use, read the enhancement's documentation (it is available in this case) and study the parameters and tables available in each user exit. Based on that information (and after consulting with Google), I chose user exit EXIT_SAPLVEDA_007 for this requirement.

Click the COMPONENTS button (Figure 6.25) and then double-click on the EXIT_SAPLVEDA_007 component.

| Enhancement | Impl | ☒ | Exp | VEDA0001 SD EDI Incoming Orders |
|---|---|---|---|---|
| Function exit | | | | EXIT_SAPLVEDA_001<br>EXIT_SAPLVEDA_002<br>EXIT_SAPLVEDA_003<br>EXIT_SAPLVEDA_004<br>EXIT_SAPLVEDA_005<br>EXIT_SAPLVEDA_006<br>EXIT_SAPLVEDA_007 |

*Figure 6.25: Components in enhancement VEDA0001*

This should open the ABAP Editor with the function module of the same name (Figure 6.26). Double-click on include ZXVEDU09 to create it.

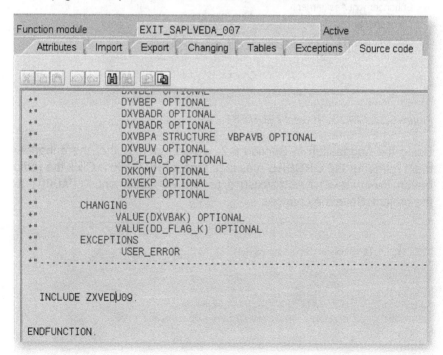

```
Function module    EXIT_SAPLVEDA_007           Active
  Attributes   Import   Export   Changing   Tables   Exceptions   Source code

*"              DXVBEP OPTIONAL
*"              DXVBADR OPTIONAL
*"              DYVBADR OPTIONAL
*"              DXVBPA STRUCTURE   VBPAVB OPTIONAL
*"              DXVBUV OPTIONAL
*"              DD_FLAG_P OPTIONAL
*"              DXKOMV OPTIONAL
*"              DXVEKP OPTIONAL
*"              DYVEKP OPTIONAL
*"      CHANGING
*"              VALUE(DXVBAK) OPTIONAL
*"              VALUE(DD_FLAG_K) OPTIONAL
*"      EXCEPTIONS
*"              USER_ERROR
*"----------------------------------------------------------------

  INCLUDE ZXVEDU09.


ENDFUNCTION.
```

*Figure 6.26: User exit EXIT_SAPLVEDA_007*

After the usual message warning about the program name and asking whether we'd like to create the include (oh yes, we would), transport prompts and other formalities, new include ZXVEDU09 opens in change mode (Figure 6.27). This is where we need to add some ABAP code.

*Figure 6.27: Include ZXVEDU09*

As you can see in the function module EXIT_SAPLVEDA_007 definition, there are many tables available. This user exit is called once per IDoc and tables can have multiple records, depending on the number of line items in the IDoc and sales order.

The table names are rather self-explanatory and are similar to the database tables (for example, DXVBAP corresponds to order line item table VBAP, DXVBEP to VBEP, etc.).

In this example, we will add some ABAP code to check if the material number supplied by the customer is valid. If not, we will look up the new material code using the old material number (MARA-BISMT) field. If we find a match, we will replace the old material number with the new one (MARA-MATNR).

```
DATA: material     TYPE matnr.

FIELD-SYMBOLS: <dxvbap_line> LIKE LINE OF xvbap.

LOOP AT dxvbap ASSIGNING <dxvbap_line>.

* Do we have a valid material number?
  SELECT SINGLE matnr INTO material
  FROM mara WHERE matnr = <dxvbap_line>-matnr.
```

```
CHECK sy-subrc NE 0.

* Is this an old material number?
  SELECT SINGLE matnr INTO material
  FROM mara WHERE bismt = <dxvbap_line>-matnr.

  IF sy-subrc = 0.
* Replace with a valid number.
    <dxvbap_line>-matnr = material.
  ENDIF.

ENDLOOP.
```

*Listing 6.2: Sample ABAP code for ZXVEDU09 include*

After activating the include, get back to the component list in transaction CMOD. It should show that the user exit has been implemented but not yet activated (Figure 6.28).

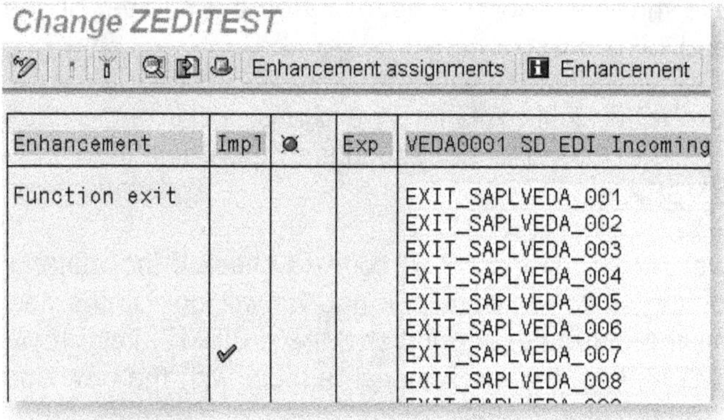

*Figure 6.28: User exit created but not active*

Activate it by clicking the ⓘ button. Note that this is where the whole project gets activated and de-activated, not just the single user exit (Figure 6.29).

Change *ZEDITEST*

✎ : 𝖎 ⎙ 🗎 ⎙ Enhancement assignments 🔢 Enhancement

| Project | | ▢ | | ZEDITEST IDoc User Exit |
|---|---|---|---|---|
| Enhancement | Impl | ▢ | Exp | LVEDF001 User exit for IDO |
| Function exit | | ▢ | | EXIT_SAPLVEDF_001 |
| | ✔ | ▢ | | EXIT_SAPLVEDF_002 |
| | | ▢ | | EXIT_SAPLVEDF_003 |
| | | ▢ | | EXIT_SAPLVEDF_004 |

| Enhancement | Impl | ▢ | Exp | VEDA0001 SD EDI Incoming O |
|---|---|---|---|---|
| Function exit | | ▢ | | EXIT_SAPLVEDA_001 |
| | | ▢ | | EXIT_SAPLVEDA_002 |
| | | ▢ | | EXIT_SAPLVEDA_003 |
| | | ▢ | | EXIT_SAPLVEDA_004 |
| | | ▢ | | EXIT_SAPLVEDA_005 |
| | | ▢ | | EXIT_SAPLVEDA_006 |
| | ✔ | ▢ | | EXIT_SAPLVEDA_007 |
| | | ▢ | | EXIT_SAPLVEDA_008 |

*Figure 6.29: Project activated*

To test this example, we need to fill in the OLD MATERIAL NUMBER field in the material master (transaction MM02), see Figure 6.30.

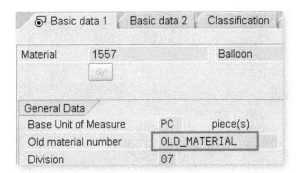

*Figure 6.30: Material master – old material number*

Note that this user exit is triggered while IDoc is processed and sales order is created, so we will not see the results in the IDoc, as we did in the outbound example (Section 6.2). The inbound IDoc will have the material number sent by the customer, but in the sales order we will see the new material number.

195

For testing, we can set a breakpoint in the user exit and then use transaction WE19 (button STANDARD INBOUND) to trigger inbound IDoc processing. (See Section 4.1 for more information on configuring an inbound interface for sales orders.)

In the debugger (Figure 6.31), we can see the old material number (OLD_MATERIAL).

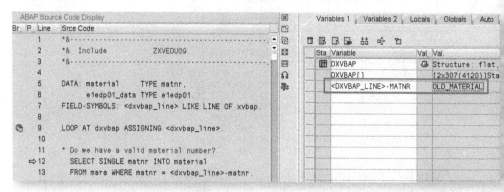

*Figure 6.31: Old material number in debugger*

After conversion in the user exit, the old material number is replaced by the new material number (1557) and the new number appears in the sales order (Figure 6.32).

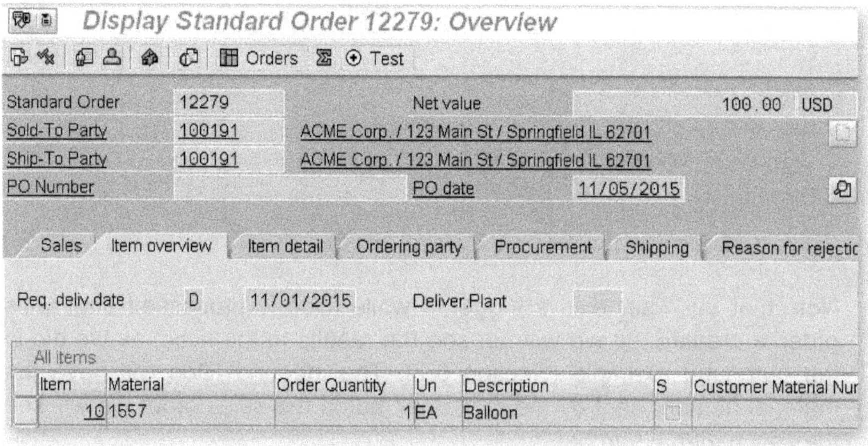

*Figure 6.32: Order created with new material number*

**Other debugging options**

Breakpoints in the user exits are also accessed while processing IDocs in transaction BD87 or running the report RBDAPP01. The report works only for the IDocs in "yellow" status.

## 6.4 Outbound file path—function module

In the outbound file interfaces (i.e. those that use XML File or File port types), it can become necessary to determine the file name dynamically. A logical directory definition (Section 2.1) already allows some flexibility, but what if your requirement is more complex?

For example, when you create XML files for the outbound invoice IDocs (as in Section 3.2), you might want the files to be placed in different directories based on the recipient. This can be achieved by creating a custom function module and adding it to the port definition.

This function module should be used with the logical directory. The parts of the file name that are to be determined by the function need to be entered as variables when assigning a physical path to the logical one in transaction FILE.

Figure 6.33 shows a path definition example that uses 3 variables:

▶ SYSID—SAP system ID, this is a system variable that fills in automatically

▶ PARAM_1—this is the "dynamic" part of the pathname that is determined by the function module

▶ FILENAME—(in this example the file name is not changed, simply use the default value)

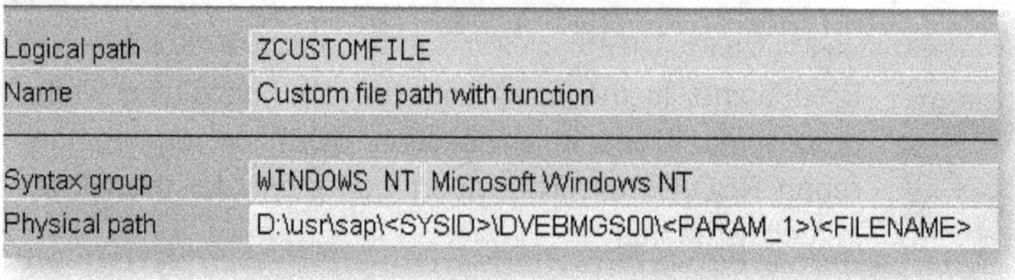

| Logical path | ZCUSTOMFILE |
|---|---|
| Name | Custom file path with function |

| Syntax group | WINDOWS NT  Microsoft Windows NT |
|---|---|
| Physical path | D:\usr\sap\<SYSID>\DVEBMGS00\<PARAM_1>\<FILENAME> |

*Figure 6.33: Logical path with variables*

SAP provides function module (FM) EDI_LPATH_CREATE_CLIENT_ DOCNUM as a sample. The custom FM example shown below (ZEDI_ FILE_PATH) was created by copying that sample function module.

In this example, simply put the IDoc receiver (CONTROL-RCVPRN) into the variable PARAMETER_1. Then call the standard function module FILE_GET_NAME_USING_PATH which "combines" the logical path (see Figure 6.33) with all the variable values and returns the physical path-name where the file will be written.

```
FUNCTION ZEDI_FILE_PATH.
*"----------------------------------------------------------------
*"*"Local Interface:
*"  IMPORTING
*"     VALUE(DATATYPE) LIKE  EDIPO-ACTRIG
*"     VALUE(DIRECTORY) LIKE  EDIPO-OUTPUTDIR
*"     VALUE(FILENAME) LIKE  EDIPO-OUTPUTFILE
*"     VALUE(CONTROL) LIKE  EDIDC STRUCTURE  EDIDC
*"  EXPORTING
*"     VALUE(PATHNAME) LIKE  EDI_PATH-PTHNAM
*"  EXCEPTIONS
*"     LOGICAL_PATH_ERROR
*"----------------------------------------------------------------

  DATA: logical_path LIKE  filepath-pathintern,
        file_name LIKE edfil-filename,
        parameter_1 TYPE c LENGTH 255.

  logical_path = directory.
  parameter_1 = control-rcvprn.
  CONDENSE parameter_1.
  file_name = filename.
```

```
CALL FUNCTION 'FILE_GET_NAME_USING_PATH'
      EXPORTING
            logical_path              = logical_path
            parameter_1               = parameter_1
            file_name                 = file_name
      IMPORTING
            file_name_with_path       = pathname
      EXCEPTIONS
            path_not_found            = 1
            missing_parameter         = 2
            operating_system_not_found = 3
            file_system_not_found     = 4
            OTHERS                    = 5.
  IF sy-subrc <> 0.
     MESSAGE ID sy-msgid TYPE sy-msgty NUMBER sy-msgno
            WITH sy-msgv1 sy-msgv2 sy-msgv3 sy-msgv4
                          RAISING logical_path_error.
  ENDIF.

ENDFUNCTION.
```

*Listing 6.3: Function module sample for outbound file name*

---

## Is there a typo?

Note that in the logical path, we use variable PARAM_1 but the function module variable name is PARAME-TER_1. It is not a typo and variable names don't actually need to match (although it would be nice if the FM parameter name matched the logical path variable name).

Only specific variables are allowed in the logical path definition. See SAP Help article "Defining Logical File Names" for the full list.

---

The logical directory (ZCUSTOMFILE in this example) and custom function module name need to be entered in the port definition (transaction WE21), see Figure 6.34.

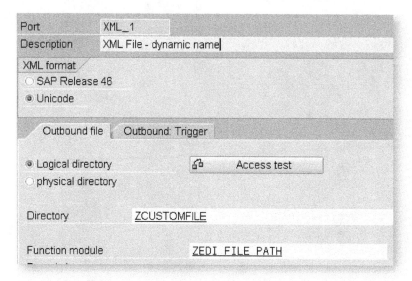

*Figure 6.34: XML file port with function module*

Note that in the custom function module, we can even use the data inside the IDoc. To do that, read the IDoc segment from the EDID4 database table and then move the data into the structure that corresponds to the segment name (e.g. E1EDKA1). This can be useful if information needed to determine the file path or name is unavailable in the IDoc control record.

# Appendix A: How and where to search for additional information

## Books

1. "ALE, EDI, & IDoc Technologies for SAP", 2nd Edition by Arvind Nagpal and John Pitlak. ISBN-10: 0761534318, ISBN-13: 008-6874534315.

I have had this book (aka "The IDoc Bible") for many years and believe it is still unrivaled by other publications on the IDoc subject. It is a dated (although not a lot changed in the IDoc world in the past 10 years, to be honest), but very detailed. My only complaint about it is that it can feel a bit too academic. It is currently out of print, but used copies can be found online or in libraries.

2. "Architecting EDI with SAP IDocs" by Emmanuel Hadzipetros. ISBN-10: 1592298710, ISBN-13: 978-1592298716.

For full disclosure—I did not read the whole book (it is 910 pages long) and only had a chance to browse through it. It is very detailed and, as the title clearly states, it is about the EDI interfaces. If you are not interested specifically in EDI then I suggest the first book instead.

3. "EDI Basics. How successful businesses connect, communicate, and collaborate around the world" by Rochelle P. Cohen. ISBN 9780989613606

This e-book is currently available for free download from OpenText website in exchange for an email address (I had no problem unsubscribing from the consequent emails). It is not written for SAP specifically, but if you are interested in learning more about the EDI concepts in general then it is a great source. This little gem of a book is relatively short (about 90 pages), well-written, and is chock full of EDI history and practical information. I enjoyed learning about the EDI world outside of the SAP walls and highly recommend this book to all the curious readers. Did I also mention it was free?

4. "Practical Workflow for SAP (3rd Edition)" by Jocelyn Dart and Susan Keohan. ISBN-10: 1493210092, ISBN-13: 978-1493210091.

If you are looking for the ultimate workflow guide I cannot imagine a more credible source than this book. The fact that it is already on the third edition speaks for itself.

## Online SAP Help and SCN

You might have noticed that several SAP Help articles were mentioned in the book. There are parts of SAP Help that make sense and are actually helpful. But, unfortunately, there are parts that are not.

SAP Community Network (SCN), on the other hand, has a lot of information in a friendlier format, but keep in mind that it is not the official SAP source. Just like any other community website, it may contain some information that is not entirely accurate.

But the good part is that both sites can be easily searched using online search engines, such as Google. In Google you can add site:sap.com to the search string to make sure that only SAP domains are searched (this includes help.sap.com and scn.sap.com). This also helps to avoid the shady websites that copy content from SCN or SAP documentation for all kinds of unsavory reasons.

When searching online also make sure to use standard SAP terminology. For example, the standard SAP term "material number" may be referred to by the business users as "part number", "SKU number", or any of 1001 other names. But when searching on SAP websites, do you think you have better chances of finding more useful information when searching for "material number" or "part number"? Hint: it is not "part number." Standard SAP terms can be found in transaction **STERM** together with their translation to multiple languages.

Great suggestions on optimizing Google search are also provided in the SCN blog *Getting the Most out of Google: Optimizing Your Search Queries* (*https://scn.sap.com/community/support/blog/2012/04/16/getting-the-most-out-of-google-optimizing-your-search-queries*) by Jason Lax.

## SCN blogs mentioned in the book

"Mapping IDocs to X12 Transactions and EDIFACT Messages"
(*http://scn.sap.com/people/community.user/blog/2009/10/12/*
*mapping-idocs-to-x12-transactions-and-edifact-messages*)
by Community User

"IDoc as Web Service" (*http://scn.sap.com/community/abap/*
*connectivity/blog/2014/09/19/idoc-as-web-service*)
by Amaresh Pani

"XML IDoc in SAP ECC without Middleware and RFC"
(*http://scn.sap.com/people/martin.dejl2/blog/2014/07/22/*
*xml-idoc-in-sap-ecc-without-middleware-and-rfc*)
by Martin Dejl

"Post IDoc to SAP ERP over HTTP from any application"
(*http://scn.sap.com/community/pi-and-soa-middleware/blog/2012/*
*01/14/post-idoc-to-sap-erp-over-http-from-any-application*)
by Grzegorz Glowacki

## SAP Notes and KBAs

There are quite a few notes and KBAs (Knowledge Base Articles) on the IDoc/ALE/EDI subject. Below are listed some note/KBA numbers that I found helpful in my previous experience or while working on this book. This is, of course, not an exhaustive list. Also, some notes are quite old and have not been updated since, keep that in mind.

At the time of this writing, SAP is piloting a new user interface for the Support portal, which is supposed to improve the note search functionality. But the note search can be challenging at times simply because the keywords in the notes are inconsistent. When searching in SAP notes and KBAs I recommend trying different variations of search terms if you are not getting the desired results. Keep in mind though that not all the subjects are covered by the SAP notes and KBAs.

44410    Integrating customer-specific fields in the material master

47071    EDI/IDoc: How is an EDI project carried out?

104606   EDI/IDoc: Mapping IDoc types to ANSI X12

116610   IDoc: Notifications from IDoc processing

127178   Questions about user exits in IDOC INVOIC01 (FI)

150017   IDoc interface: Documentation and training

420562   REP: Reducing the scope of data for change pointers

456127   FAQ: Electronic Data Interchange (EDI) in purchasing

513454   'REP: High performance operation with change pointers'

521427   FAQ: IDocs for goods movements

545626   FAQ: Data transfer problems (MATMAS)

551035   IDOC overview in FI

701597   Documentation for the CL_HTTP_IDOC_XML_REQUEST class

747631   Some tips when testing idoc_input_orders

752194   Serialization of IDoc processing

753153   FAQ: Customer functions in IDOC_INPUT_ORDERS

754333   Segments are not updated during IDOC inbound processing

# Appendix B: The sticky note version of the book

This is a quick reference of the transaction codes and reports related to the scenarios described in the book.

## Common elements of the IDoc interfaces

WE21    Port definition

WE20    Partner profile

BD54    Logical system

BD64    Distribution model (for logical system)

## Change pointers

BD61    Activate change pointers globally

BD50    Change pointers by message type

BD52    Fields that trigger change pointers

BD21    Create IDoc from change pointers

## General IDoc transactions

WE02/WE05    IDoc display

WE09/WE10    Search in IDoc segments

WLF_IDOC     IDoc Monitor (available starting from EHP5)

BD87         IDoc processing

WE60         IDoc documentation

WE19         Test tool

WE42 / WE64   Process codes

## Other transactions

NACE   Output configuration

SM59   RFC connection (for RFC port)

AL11   Files on the application server

CG3Y   Download file from the application server

CG3Z   Upload file to the application server

FILE   Logical directory names

## Reports

RBDAPP01   Process inbound IDocs

RBDMANIN / RBDMANI2      Process inbound IDocs in error

RBDMIDOC   Create IDoc from change pointers (same as transaction BD21)

RBDCPCLR   Clean-up processed change pointers

RSNAST00   Process output (NAST table)

RSEOUT00   Process outbound IDocs

RSEXARCA / RSEXARCB      Archive IDocs

RSEXARCD   Delete archived IDocs

**You have finished the book.**

# A The Author

Jelena Perfiljeva is a Technical SAP Analyst at Elster Solutions, LLC in North Carolina.

Since her SAP career started by accident 10 years ago, she has worked as an ABAP programmer and general SAP problem solver in the whole-sale, professional service, and manufacturing industries. Her duties included implementation and support of numerous EDI and IDoc interfaces.

Jelena's lack of any official SAP credentials has not prevented her from becoming an SAP Mentor, an SCN blogger, and a speaker at international SAP events. She was SCN Member of the Month in April 2013.

When she is not debugging SAP or answering questions on SCN, she enjoys using Google for finding new food recipes to test on her unsuspecting family members.

# B Index

# C   Disclaimer

This publication contains references to the products of SAP SE.

SAP, R/3, SAP NetWeaver, Duet, PartnerEdge, ByDesign, SAP BusinessObjects Explorer, StreamWork, and other SAP products and services mentioned herein as well as their respective logos are trademarks or registered trademarks of SAP SE in Germany and other countries.

Business Objects and the Business Objects logo, BusinessObjects, Crystal Reports, Crystal Decisions, Web Intelligence, Xcelsius, and other Business Objects products and services mentioned herein as well as their respective logos are trademarks or registered trademarks of Business Objects Software Ltd. Business Objects is an SAP company.

Sybase and Adaptive Server, iAnywhere, Sybase 365, SQL Anywhere, and other Sybase products and services mentioned herein as well as their respective logos are trademarks or registered trademarks of Sybase, Inc. Sybase is an SAP company.

SAP SE is neither the author nor the publisher of this publication and is not responsible for its content. SAP Group shall not be liable for errors or omissions with respect to the materials. The only warranties for SAP Group products and services are those that are set forth in the express warranty statements accompanying such products and services, if any. Nothing herein should be construed as constituting an additional warranty.

# More Espresso Tutorials Books

Boris Rubarth:

## First Steps in ABAP®

- ▶ Step-by-Step instructions for beginners
- ▶ Comprehensive descriptions and code examples
- ▶ A guide to create your first ABAP application
- ▶ Tutorials that provide answers to the most commonly asked programming questions

*http://5015.espresso-tutorials.com*

Antje Kunz:

## SAP® Legacy System Migration Workbench (LSMW)

- ▶ Data Migration (No Programming Required)
- ▶ SAP LSMW Explained in Depth
- ▶ Detailed Practical Examples
- ▶ Tips and Tricks for a Successful Data Migration

*http://5051.espresso-tutorials.com*

Darren Hague:

## Universal Worklist with SAP NetWeaver® Portal

- ▶ Learn to easily execute business tasks using Universal Worklist
- ▶ Find in-depth advice on how to mak SAP workflows and alerts available
- ▶ Learn how to Include 3rd party workflows in SAP NetWeaver Portal

*http://5076.espresso-tutorials.com*

Michal Krawczyk:

## SAP® SOA Integration

▶ Tools for Monitoring SOA Scenarios

▶ Forward Error Handling (FEH) and Error Conflict Handler (ECH)

▶ SAP Application Interface Framework (AIF) Customization Best Practices

▶ Detailed Message Monitoring and Reprocessing Examples

*http://5077.espresso-tutorials.com*

Dominique Alfermann, Stefan Hartmann, Benedikt Engel:

## SAP® HANA Advanced Modeling

▶ Data modeling guidelines and common test approaches

▶ Modular solutions to complex requirements

▶ Information view performance optimization

▶ Best practices and recommendations

*http://4110.espresso-tutorials.com*

Kathi Kones:

## SAP List Viewer (ALV) – A Practical Guide for ABAP Developers

▶ Learn how to write a basic SAP ALV program

▶ Walk through the object-oriented control framework and function modules

▶ Get tips on adding sorting and grouping features

▶ Dive into how to add editable fields, events, and layout variants

*http://5112.espresso-tutorials.com*

www.ingramcontent.com/pod-product-compliance
Lightning Source LLC
Chambersburg PA
CBHW052144070326
40689CB00050B/2009